COBRA COMBAT

BY ROBERT E. CASE
LT. COL. USAF

authorHOUSE®

AuthorHouse™
1663 Liberty Drive
Bloomington, IN 47403
www.authorhouse.com
Phone: 1-800-839-8640

Published by AuthorHouse 3/18/2013

ISBN: 978-1-4817-2275-9 (sc)
ISBN: 978-1-4817-2276-6 (hc)
ISBN: 978-1-4817-2277-3 (e)

Library of Congress Control Number: 2013903952

PREFACE

I am not attempting to write history and in some ways I am maybe writing fiction. This is not history as recorded rather it is history as recalled.

Much of my records and pictures are lost in mysterious ways and airplane numbers, squadron members, and exact dates; are long since forgotten although the internet has refreshed some of the data.

This account is intended to reflect the happenings and events as I would, and did, tell them to men like me when we met and swapped lies. We called those sessions hanger flying.

In the many years since the big war ended I have met many interesting men with interesting stories. Some may appear in this effort.

Over the years many people have urged me to put my experiences on paper. I have felt that these experiences are commonplace and were in kind with the millions of men and women who participated in that war and thus unworthy of note. However I have read that the World War 2 generation is now passing to the tune of 20 - 25,000 a month and as I have been told – if I don't write it down - it never happened.

Therefore for all the men with which I served, now it has happened.

Robert E Case served this country for 26 years through two wars. In the "big one" he was awarded the Distinguished Flying Cross, 13 awards of the Air Combat Medal, unit citations, campaign ribbons, and others. His career spans from the Army Air Corps where the front line fighters were just breaking 300 miles per hour, through the USAF with fighters capable of Mach 3+.

When asked the stories of the 13 Air Combat Medals his response was that he ate his oatmeal. When asked why he was awarded the DFC his response was he didn't complain about eating his oatmeal. Getting this story has been a long and arduous process spanning well over 50 years.

Those that actually fought the enemies of democracy seem to see no reason to tell their story, they just did their job. The phenomenal historical impacts of their effort don't make much impression on them. They were just doing what they were trained to do, along with sixteen million other men and women, and there was nothing special about them – well according to them. History has proved them different.

They persisted through the most horrific combat conditions, suffered under extreme climate, primitive medical support and technology, and routine lack of supply. They endured disease, malaria, dysentery; poisonous snakes and bugs; monsoon and typhoon; and yet every day they mounted their warplanes and rose to challenge the Imperial Japanese Naval and Army Air Forces.

The pilots of this time flew three to seven combat sorties a day for weeks at a time; navigating across hundreds of miles of ocean to strike at the enemy, oft times with faulty navigation equipment - only to find their own air strip in flames from Japanese attack upon their return. Robert's air group fought a numerically superior, better trained and better equipped enemy, most having years of combat experience, flying aircraft that were in many respects better than the front line equipment available to the Americans.

Robert and those of his class fought when the outcome of the war was still in doubt, when the enemy was not a desperate defeated foe strangled by lack of supply and crippled by routine defeat. God owned Heaven, but who owned the sky was still under discussion. By the time he left the Pacific theater the sky had clear tints of red, white, and blue.

It would be another year before Japan surrendered, but the writing was on the wall.

Years ago when the gray eagles would gather and the beverages started to flow and tongues would slightly loosen, rare glimpses of this history as told by the men that made it could be heard by hiding off the stairwell. Bits and pieces do not a story make. Finally the story is told.

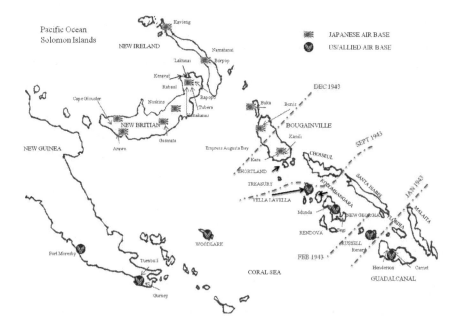

TABLE OF CONTENTS

PREAMBLE TO WAR

I was born in Brooklyn, N.Y. - and as the song goes - on a cold and frosty morn in January 1916. I mention that not because I can't think of a start point for this story but rather with that birth date I was normally the oldest man in any unit to which I was ever assigned. Due to health issues with my mother, my father moved the family to the countryside in New Jersey where I arrived on my fifth birthday. I was accompanied by two elder brothers, an elder sister and the baby sister.

I don't know exactly when I became infatuated with aircraft and the thought of flying. I remember I had seen airplanes just before leaving New York. An older boy from down the street had taken me to Canarsey to watch the pilots from WWI fly passenger hops in DH4 Jennies. I was mesmerized by the noise and rush of those little birds and think that was when I decided I would become a pilot.

In Jersey we lived close to the Lakehurst Naval Air Station (N.A.S.) and I saw lots of flying from there. All the big dirigibles were stationed there and all activity stopped – yard work or school work – when one of the Navy's warships flew overhead. I got to see history made – though didn't know it at the time when the naval warship USS Macon (ZRS5) was launched out of Ohio and stationed at LNAS from 1933 - 35.

The concept for that time was that these airships would carry small fighter planes (FC9 Sparrow Hawks) and bombs and be the aircraft carriers of the future. The Macon ran several successful missions intercepting several warships including the USS Huston carrying President Franklin D Roosevelt on his way to Hawaii. The technological wonder of her time; the USS Macon was destroyed in a storm on Feb 13, 1935 and effectively ended the Navy's experiment with rigid airships. Lakehurst was still used for non-rigid dirigibles and a parachute school.

Of course the most famous airship to land at LNAS was the German Zeppelin the Hindenburg. A routine landing in May of 1937 ended in disaster as is well recorded and the loss of 35 people which was huge news in 1937. I did not see the ship but my elder brother Henry was on the cleanup crew once the Nazi's allowed US naval folks to clean up the remains of the ship.

Of course there were plenty of biplane fighters and bombers that would loiter overhead and they too attracted a crowd of observers – none more interested than I.

I attended grammar school in the country. Three rooms, a wood stove, a shed out back, and a well. That was the entire makeup of the school. The older boys got to chop wood for the fire and the younger kids helped the two ladies maintain the classrooms and tidy the grounds. In my later years coal was delivered to the school and then we elder boys got to shovel coal. There was a dipper in the water bucket that all grades got to drink from and of course the little house out back served as the privy. We learned to write on slate using chalk and had to share the classroom with assorted grades. Grades 1-4 were in one half and 5-8 in the second half. My part of New Jersey hadn't yet passed the primitive living style and one could easily imagine we were in school on the frontier in the 1860's.

The state highway passed close to the school. It was a two lane roadway that had crushed gravel rolled into the earth. It was better than the two tracks it replaced as the main highway however rain and sleet turned the roadbed into a mud pit just as surely as if there was no gravel. It was designed to handle the high volume of traffic – 10 to 20 cars and wagons per hour and survive the winters and summers until the next work gang came through and repaved the roadway. It was an exceptional road compared to the wheel tracks in the Jersey sand where they crossed the woods and qualified for secondary roads. Most of the towns sported either brick or cobble stone for their main streets although there were plenty of dirt roads in the towns as well.

My mother's health steadily declined while we were in New Jersey, the move to the country did not have the desired curative effect. As her condition was not yet fully diagnosed she was selected to enter a sanitarium for observation. We would visit every Sunday after Mass but there were times when she just never woke up. My father resigned from the New York Police Department and took up the trade of a plumber. He really had no formal training and what technical knowledge he gained was from books in the library and practice around the farm. He operated a successful business in that we didn't starve and the farm was paid off but that is pretty much the limit of his success.

Mom passed away before the great depression although her passing was greatly depressing. I was just staring 8th grade and the family had to make major changes in our lifestyle. Just as my mother passed the banks went into failure. My father stood outside the bank where he had his money day after day trying to get into his accounts. The banks would open for a few minutes a day and then immediately close their doors. They were in a bad way as they had over loaned their assets and could not collect their funds before the runs. Needless to say my father lost all his money. We were fortunate that the farm was paid off and the latest crop of stew chickens was paid for. Those stew chickens and pop's pluming jobs pretty much saw us through the first year of the Depression.

There is really nothing exceptional in our survival of the Great Depression – our chickens failed - there was some kind of blight on the eggs and we ended up losing all of those. However we did have a 22 caliber rifle and a lot of rabbits and squirrels in our neck of the woods. The rabbits attempted to eat our vegetable garden and eventually I pretty much ensured any rabbit eating our vegetables ended up in our stew pot. It got to the point that pop rationed the bullets giving me two rounds a day. If I took my time and aimed well we had meat for our dinner – if not we had beans and vegetables in the summer.

High school was by contract. I lived close to the county line so I had to go to the nearest school which was Lakewood, H.S. I was like most other kids of the time and wanted to be on the varsity football team but at 100 pounds soaking wet there was not much hope for me. Coach Russell Wright an All American out of West Virginia became the head coach of the Lakewood High School Football team. He saw me and a couple of my buddies hanging around the field and asked us if we wanted to play ball. My buddy Elwood Kingsley told him we were only freshmen and wouldn't stand a chance against the big varsity folks. That did not discourage Coach Wright, he said he was building a freshman team and wanted all of us to come out. He would run the varsity practice on one end of the field and the freshman team on the other end of the field. We did not have a JV at the time.

The freshmen reported to the gym and picked up our issue of football equipment – a mishmash of whalebone pants, leather helmets with a steel plate and cloth padding, and our cleats. There were some shoulder pads but most didn't use them as they were more a nuisance than a protection. The ones available were again whalebone guards with cloth under wrappings and canvas straps. They were uncomfortable and pretty much ineffective.

I believe there were 12 of us freshmen and the coach had us warm up with the varsity in the back. Then the varsity went to one end of the field and the coach told the team captain what plays he wanted run and how to conduct practice while he worked with the freshmen. Coach Wright came to our end of the field – gave us a few tips and some techniques to use and then had us line up and smash into each other. There was a broken leg, one dislocated shoulder, and a broken wrist. That was the end of the freshman team that year.

My father was in a near fatal accident and he couldn't work for over two years. We barely subsisted through that period. My elder sister married and moved out of the house and my elder brothers attempted to find work. As a sophomore in school my father wanted me to stay in school but things were tight. Luckily I had a good friend in Elwood – they were not hit as hard as my household and Mrs. Kingsley told Elwood to bring me home from school with him and I got a pretty good feed. Often there was "too much" food so I was "forced" to take some extra biscuits and fresh bread with some meat to help out with my little sister and my dad.

Sophomore year I went out for track – not that I was anything special but I could run the 100 yard dash – I had to pass the meanest Doberman in the town on my way home from school and often he was loose. I would have complained to the lady who owned him but never had the nerve to go back and say anything. But I didn't get bit too often so I must have been pretty fast. That track work would bode me ill in the future although I didn't know it at the time.

With a letter in Track and Field under my belt I made the varsity football team my Junior and Senior years in high school. This was during the height of the depression and my pop was often out of town trying to get work. I was accountable for my little sister and we made do with what was in the house. We lived alone and in the dark because lamp fuel was expensive. My varsity football was often the only thing that kept me in school and in some cases was the only way I got a good meal, travel team was fed on the road and the coach always ensured I got a double helping. We played 11 men back then. If you started you played offense and defense, there was no platoon efforts like today. I played offensive end but I never got to catch a pass only block, and on defense I played defensive end or tackle depending on the scheme. Lakewood lost one game my junior year in 1932 and went undefeated in my senior year in 1933 – earning the Central Jersey Championship. The two years on the varsity football team was the best thing that ever happened to me. The coach was a sincere and dedicated man who kept me and other struggling boys in school.

Graduating in June of 1934 I found the coach had obtained two scholarships for Elwood and me. Neither of us had the slightest intent of going to yet another 4 years of school – we needed to get out into the world and start earning some money so without a second thought we turned down the offers.

The first place I applied for employment was with the United States Army Air Corps. I took my high school diploma to the nearest recruiter and was promptly denied – they had college men waiting to make the waiting list why would they care about a 100 pound 18 year old kid even if I did have a diploma – which was rare in those days as most kids did not finish high school.

I wasn't done yet. I had a cousin in New York who heard about my plight. She was married to a big time lawyer who was a personal friend of Royal S. Copeland a US Senator from New York. I figured I'd pull some strings and be flying within the month. According to my cousin, Senator Copeland did make a phone call but that didn't do any good.

The air service was only taking college graduates. At the suggestion of the recruiter I wrote a letter to the USAAC and requested that I be assigned to flight school. I wrote that letter in July of 1934 and heard nothing further.

I managed to get in the Civilian Conservation Corps CCCs that Roosevelt got going for all the young men that were out of work. The pay was $30 per month, $5 of which you got to keep for your personal things and $25.00 sent automatically to my family. That $25 was all my father and sister had to live on for the month. The work was horrendous but I was working with other young men my age and we got food and a tent to sleep in so it was a great improvement over what a lot of folks were used to. You had to commit to either a 6 month or 1 year tour and it was run just like Army boot camp. I signed up for a 6 month tour and was assigned to Fairy Stone State park in Patrick County Virginia named after the rare mineral crosses that cover the park. We built roads, bridges, cabins, campgrounds, outhouses, trails and parking lots. I went back in 2010 and many of the structures I worked on were still there.

I left the CCCs and went back to Lakewood where I did odd jobs and sold fire wood. I was in the woods chopping some dead trees when I saw one of my high school buddies walking toward me. Milt was on break from his job as a waiter at Newman High School – an exclusive school for the well to do for which Lakewood had more than its fair share. Apparently the assistant chef was fired for stealing food and a position was opening that very moment. If I wanted the job he'd vouch for me.

I raced back to my farm, threw my wood into the wood pile and raced to the well to wash off some of the sweat and stink of chopping wood on a hot New Jersey day. Milt had been good on his promise and had put in a good word for me and I started working that evening as an assistant chef. I made $235 a month and got to eat all that I could stuff in my face. Laundry was free as was the room. For two years this was what I called heaven. My father had recovered from his wounds from the car wreck and checked out some books on stationary plant engineering – power plants for buildings. He got a job in Florida and moved down there with my baby sister.

I wanted to learn a trade and eventually moved off to become a sheet metal man – I built the ductwork for the heating and that new technology the wealthy were obtaining, air cooling as we called air conditioning. I was making enough money now that I could send home a literal fortune, buy a car and buy flying lessons - since that Air Corps thing was not working out for me. I finally got a job as a sheet metal man's helper and the few years before the war I progressed to Junior Mechanic.

I still had a passion for flight and had paid the $3.00 for a 5 minute flight in one of the old Jennies. I was impressed; this is what I wanted to do as a life passion. I went to the flying school and for $7.00 an hour learned to fly on Stearmans, Pipers, and a Ryan. I managed to get pretty good rather quickly which was not a good thing for my flight instructor because lessons were $7.00, rentals were $5.00.

During those years I progressed from $3.00 a day to $14.00 a day. There wasn't any withholding tax so I was now living well with plenty to eat. My boss got a contract with the government building housing at Fort Drum and I had to move up north where I lived in a boarding house run by a kindly matron with a very attractive 18 year old daughter.

I was no different than any other guy and I wanted a car worse than anything else. I was driving a junker so I could get to work - a twenty five dollar Hupmobile and felt it was time to move up to a real machine. One day I saw a little '39 Pontiac Coup in a dealer's sales lot and it looked perfect. It had a radio and a heater, which I had never seen before in a car and was an astounding dark green with tan interior. I had to have it. I gave the dealer all I had which was $300 dollars and I was the proudest Pontiac Coup owner in the world.

That evening I drove it home and parked in front of my rooming house. I note here that there was a lovely 18-year-old daughter living there and I wanted that car clearly displayed. I had been in the house for a couple of months and wanted to ensure she saw just how prosperous I had become.

I walked into the house and checked the little table where the landlady put the mail. There was a business envelope there addressed to me. I was somewhat surprised but opened it. In large letters at the top it said

7

GREETINGS:

Having submitted yourself to a Local Board composed of your neighbors for the purpose of determining your availability for training and service in the armed forces of the United States, you are hereby notified that you have now been selected for training and service in the ARMY. You will therefore report to the Local Board named above at 20 Court St., Freehold, New Jersey at 8:45 am on the Thirteenth of February 1941.

I had heard about the draftees but paid little attention. And now literally I was one. My boss tried to exempt me based on critical war work, Lend Lease was already flowing and everyone knew the nation needed to get ready. That appeal fell on deaf ears.

I drove the little coup to my sister and her husband's house near our farm. They asked if they could use it and I never saw it again. That was February 1941.

I was in the second draft. I was sent to Camp Dix and was wearing my new clothes; a brand new camel hair coat, blue pin stripped suit, and brand new, 8 dollar pair of wing tip shoes. I had just bought those clothes with the high pay I had finally achieved and wanted to make a good impression on the Army folks. Looking rather dapper I thought for sure I was a shoe in for an immediate promotion. I really didn't understand how the Army worked yet.

Since we didn't have uniforms to work in we had to work in the clothes we wore when we were sworn-in. I was assigned to the coal and ash detail- and upon reflection – I think some corporal did that on purpose. I leave the remainder of that to your imagination.

The commander there was General Lear. He got in trouble with the press because he disciplined some soldiers for whistling at girls through the fence. The press called him Yoo Hoo Ben Lear from that day on. He was an exceptionally impressive looking man but that is all I can recall of him. I was not in his command long and he didn't really have much to do with a mere private.

In only a couple of weeks we were shipped to Ft. Knox, Kentucky for Recruit Drill. This is what would now be termed boot camp but at that time the Army was still experimenting on the best way to train troops. Some folks went directly to units and it was the unit's responsibility to train them, however that was not efficient and the Army was very much into efficiency. My Recruit Drill taught me all the basics, how to wear the uniform, how to march, marksmanship, care and cleaning and even how to brush my teeth.

Basic Training ended when the '41 maneuvers commenced. I was assigned to the Sixteenth Engineers, First Armored Division (Regular). Before leaving for the maneuvers in Louisiana, Lieutenant Colonel Patton came over from Fort Bragg to visit our unit. The Army was about to take a Cadre from us to activate another Armored Division and Patton was to coordinate the effort of constructing an entire new armored division.

One day we were to practice a river crossing under simulated fire. We marched out in the dark and Lieutenant Colonel Patton marched 14 miles to the Salt River beside me without ever saying a word to me or anyone else. We engineers were going to breach the enemy fortifications and build a bridge under combat conditions so other units could cross the river and thus win the battle and conclude the exercise. Naturally with all the effort and money involved in a maneuver this complex, there were to be plenty of congressional and other very important visitors watching the show.

The demonstration was a disaster. One of our NCO's tripped over a root, in the dark while going down a steep slope and fell into a boat. That was during the 'silent' approach phase. A tremendous boom along with a horrible clatter resulted from his personal equipment slamming around in the metal boat, and those folks carrying the boat dropped it as it slid down the hill. His cussing didn't help the silent maneuvers any either.

That surprise was ended and the opposing team opened up with blanks and flares. We were annihilated. The Secretary of War was there for the demonstration amongst the other VIPs and I imagine Major General Magruder, our Division Commander must have had heart failure. It was the last I ever saw of Patton in person and I never saw that NCO again. I wonder if they took him out and shot him.

WE GET READY FOR WAR

When the Sixteenth Engineer Battalion (armored) got on the road with all authorized men and equipment it stretched 24 miles. Travel interval called Road Discipline was rigid. Fifty yards was the minimal distance between vehicles for combat maneuver but the "administrative" space between vehicles had to be provided so civilian traffic could move through the columns.

When the column moved through a southern town motorcycle troops would go ahead and control the local traffic because there was no stopping the heavy equipment quickly. Most southern towns had a square in the center of the town and in those days all highways went through the business district of towns and cities. The business people wanted travelers to do some business there and leave money with the stores..

Our tanks were big M3 Grant tanks in the heavy regiments. Grants were the interim tank until the M4 Shermans could be fielded. The Grant had a 75mm gun in a sponson in the hull, a 37mm high velocity gun in the turret and in some versions (called a Lee) had a .50 caliber machinegun in a smaller turret mounted on the 37mm gun turret. The 75mm gun was accurate to 3000 yards and the 37mm good to 1500 yards. The Grant fought well in the deserts of North Africa and got a reputation for having good armor, mechanical reliability, and heavy fire power. That it could fire on two targets independently and at the same time spelled the demise of some German armor in the deserts.

Our column moved at a controlled speed of 20 miles per hour, but our tanks were not designed for that kind of speed on improved roadways and it was apparently a difficult task to control the heavy tanks while going around the square. One of our tanks swung wide and hit a parked car, a 27 Ford, and the right track climbed up on the car and squashed it like it was a bug under foot. Oil ran out of it on the pavement and what was left of that car literally needed to be scraped off the roadway. Luckily no one was in the car and no one was hurt. Still 27 tons of steel was hard to control on those macadam roadways.

It was funny to see what that tank did to the light car; but there were many such incidents with many more to come as the services expanded, and unfortunately, some of the incidents did cause injury. It would be years before streets would be void of uniformed men and military vehicles.

We camped out in the forests where no heavy traffic had been for many years. I was in a recon unit and the maps I saw were dated 1912. The movement of troops excited the wild life and snakes and wild pigs became a problem. Rattlesnakes were huge some measuring over 15 feet long and stretched across the road. Cotton mouths and moccasins came out of the rivers and ponds and would attack the unwary soldier. There were many attacks and there were real casualties caused by the snakes.

One man from the 80th Recon became hysterical and we had to restrain him. Others had to be forced to sleep on the ground, which no one wanted to do because snakes tended to "cuddle up" with the warm bodies at night. A ten foot rattle snake is a terrifying thing to see and the snakes were frightened by the sudden incursion of endless people and vehicles. That made them much more aggressive and much more dangerous. There was a rattle snake skin on display in a taxidermist shop window that measured thirteen feet long and I saw that with my own eyes. It had the rattles still on it.

My company commander was a man who had captured snakes for a company who made medicine to counter-act poisonous snake bites. He instructed us to tell him if we saw a Cotton Mouth or Moccasin because he wanted to catch it. This man had only worked with Copper Heads and Rattle Snakes up north. One of the southern men told him to be careful because Moccasins were not like rattlers and would come after you. The Captain laughed and said "I can handle any snake God put on this earth."

A short time later we were down in a deep swamp washing cloths and bathing. I happened to look up and saw a Moccasin lying on a tree limb over the water. He looked plenty big to me but then I think all snakes look dangerous and usually vacate any area snakes are present. I did watch this one as he was a 100 yards or so downstream from us and this snake would drop off the limb on frogs and catch them. It was the strangest thing I ever saw. I told one of the guys to get the old man which he did. The Captain came down and had a short stick with the forked end on it. He intended to pin the snake to the branch and capture the thing for his collection.

The snake seemed to be frozen on the limb and didn't make any move to escape. When the little stick got close to him, it was like a flash, he moved so suddenly climbing right up the stick. Moccasins can bite and don't have to strike like many other snakes. The Captain avoided the attack but was so startled he threw the stick in the river and ran. To this day I believe he would have given ten years of his life if he hadn't shown that abject terror in front of his men.

The Battalion Surgeon was a scientist who had worked in one of the museums in N.Y. He had published a notice that if anyone captured a Coral Snake he wanted it to send to his Museum. Some of the men did get one for him in north Florida and it was after the capture that they learned the Coral Snake is one of the most deadly snakes in the US. They were very rare.

My job all through the '41 maneuvers was as driver for the recon officer. He had to check all roads and bridges to make sure they could carry our vehicles. Some of our equipment weighed 12,000 pounds and of course our tanks were 27 tons. The Army provided us with maps and routes and special measuring equipment and formulas to calculate the bridge structural strength. Mostly I just hung out in the vehicle while the recon officer marked bridges on the maps and decided where tanks could cross.

My vehicle was a Command and Reconnaissance Car (C&R). It was an open, two seat, four wheel drive car of very heavy construction easily capable of sitting six people although the normal compliment was four. The official title of the car was the Dodge VC1 which had a flat head 6 cylinder with 80 hp at 3000 rpms. Some 2200 were produced up till 1941. The VC2s were designed with radios but my car did not have an organic radio although we did mount a portable radio in the back occasionally. It had a 116 inch wheel base and superb ground clearance. Because of its light weight and excellent terrain capabilities it could go places other vehicles simply could not go. Any place the tanks and guns were to go, my recon car went first. We made endless road marches, reports, and bridge grading. By the end of summer we had gotten very proficient at that.

By that time there were several hundred thousand troops spread across East Texas, Louisiana, Alabama and North Florida. Much of that force was moved to the Carolinas in the fall. I use to wonder what it took to feed, clothe and supply all the units when they were all in motion. Who could coordinate such detail? All this logistics was done with paper and pencil and then transferred to some standard form on a typewriter which was hand delivered or wired to a supply depot. Somehow food was delivered on time, gas arrived on schedule and maintenance parts managed to appear when needed.

No matter where we were, on a march, in a night cantonment, or pulled into a base camp the all-important personal mail reached us no matter where we were including swamps and uncharted forests. That service never failed during my entire career and never has there been a better motivator for the troops than to receive a letter from mom and pop or that special one from the sweetie at home. Mail call was the highlight of any day.

One event that caused me some discomfort happened at the end of a long and hard day of driving. We arrived at the cook's camp and the Lieutenant had me stop there. We were served even though chow had long since been over. He then talked to several other officers. The Lieutenant came back to where I was sitting and told me he would have to stay where we were that night. He would catch up to me in the morning. My instructions were to get into whatever column was passing and go to some other increment of our company further down the road.

I did that and just kept going. It finally dawned on me that something was badly amiss. I saw one of our other company's ID signs beside the road so I pulled in there. I was about out of gas at that time, anyway. I got to the First Sergeant who thought a moment and then took me to the Company Commander Captain Waters and I had had enough to do with him that he remembered me.

"What's the trouble soldier?" he asked me and I explained my circumstance. He thought for some time before he said "Private. There isn't any way I can communicate with your outfit. We will gas you up and you make the decision on whether to stay here or go back tonight."

I started back and then realized I wouldn't be able to stay awake so I pulled into a secluded place and put my sleeping bag down and went to sleep. It was late but sometime later something woke me. It took a while but I knew it was something I had never heard before. I eased out of my bag and sneaked to the edge of my cover. It was a sight I will never forget.

It was Horse Cavalry as far as I could see in either direction. The horses were silent. No snorting or anything of that sort. The road was dirt so hooves were also muted. I watched them easing by for about an hour. That sight will stay with me forever. In all that time there was no sound that could carry past the side of the road. The discipline in that unit was absolute and a sense of pride choked me up; I will never forget that scene. It must have been a Regiment.

Later I was glad to know they would never be used in combat. The awful damage the automatic weapons could do to them gave me a sick feeling of apprehension. All units were converting to mechanized equipment at that time. After the war I learned my wife's cousin was in the horse Cavalry and was captured by Germans in a battle of some sort and I got to serve with dismounted Cavalry on Woodlark Island in the Pacific.

That morning I fired up the recon car and got back to the point where I started from. The Lieutenant was having breakfast. He started to rake me over the coals but I said, "Lieutenant if you recall your order I did what you commanded and sir privates don't interpret orders." He laughed and there was no further issue.

I had another conflict with a Lieutenant. I was instructed to take the water cans to the purification unit, one of the many tasks I had to perform when not actually doing road and route reconnaissance. As I was leaving a Lieutenant jumped in and said he would ride with me as he had nothing better to do. He immediately started to describe all his conquests of the ladies in the area and proved that even then not all commissioned officers were gentlemen. I really didn't want to hear his bragging but privates don't usually tell Lieutenants what they would prefer to do.

The guy had thrown his hat into the back of the car and when I filled up the cans and worked them back into position in the back the hat wasn't seen. When we returned and I started to unload the water cans he was looking for his hat. He found it under one of the cans it was soaked and cans had ridden on it crushing the bill.

He started to rave at me saying I would pay for his hat. Now my parents following pretty much the custom of the time had strict injunctions against profanity. Anyone in the house that made a slip or violated that injunction got either the belt or the wooden spoon, and in some cases both. Profanity was not tolerated and did not become part of my language; therefore, I lack the vocabulary to describe that Lieutenant and what happened to my First Sergeant.

The First Sergeant heard the disorder where there was supposed to be silence and came over asking the Lieutenant what the trouble was. The Lieutenant described the event and used very foul language when referring to me. He also said I would pay for the hat. The Sergeant told the officer I was not responsible for his personal property and further he would have to apologize for the language he used.

The two men used hard words during the remainder of the conversation which eventually ended up in the Commanding Officer's hooch. The officer was shipped out with a reprimand but the First Sergeant was busted to private after we returned to Ft. Knox at the end of the maneuvers.

I thought this was grossly unfair but enlisted did not talk back to the commissioned types. Period. Never ever. The military justice system was a system designed to ensure the officer maintained full control and command of his people no matter how unfair it may have been. To be fair most of the officers were decent men well educated and well spoken. In my experience very few were as ignorant and obnoxious as this one.

P-39 Airacobras and P-36 Hawks were used to simulate attacks on us. They would come by at high speeds and also, unannounced, spray tear gas. Woe be it to anyone who didn't have his gas mask. You never would be caught without it twice. The spraying of the troops was one way to ensure the troops reacted to the air attack drills.

I later got in trouble myself with the same kind of mission. I was flying a P-51D-35. We were doing the same exercise to some troops in training that the 39s did to us; however, someone crossed in front of me just as we sprayed and I flew right into a track of 100% tear gas. I lost all my vision and called my wingman to keep me level. He did that and I opened the canopy to air out. It took some time for my vision to clear. I won't try to describe the irritation of the gas in my eyes.

During the exercises in the Carolinas we had a rest period outside Rock Hill. I put on my best cloths and went to town. At the edge of town I saw some Piper Cubs flying so I walked over to watch as I had about 60 hours of flight time in a similar model. There were many spectators watching the small planes twist and turn over the field. One was an older man standing a few yards from me who finally came over to say hello.

He asked me what I was doing that evening to which I said I didn't have anything to do. I intended to walk around a bit and then go back to camp. He said he would like me to come home with him for supper. I thanked him but said I better not. I was as ripe as a man can get. I didn't want to offend his wife. He just laughed and said it won't be the first time because he had come home from hunting just like I was.

I went with him to a tidy little bungalow and met his family. That was a lovely, refined lady with two teenage daughters. Now I felt even worse. The lady wasn't the least bit bashful. She said "we are first going to get you more comfortable." She told her husband to get me his robe and one of the girls to fill the tub while the lady finished getting supper. I washed several months of dirt and sweat off of my hide and can't tell how good that felt I shaved with the man's razor and left the bathroom squeaky clean as the saying goes. I put on the clothes the man loaned me and walked out to the dining room.

When I came out the girls giggled and one said; "mother he's handsome. Can we keep him?" They teased me that way all through the evening. Supper was a treat and after that we gathered around and the dad showed me his pictures which inspired many questions from the family. The man had seen a great deal of battle in WWI.

The girls brought out his medals. They were very proud of their dad and the lady smiled at me when the kids showed them off. Like most true warriors I have met in my time he didn't have much to say about the actual fighting and how he earned those medals.

The evening ended much too soon for my tastes but it was getting dark and I needed to be on my way. My summer uniform had been washed and ironed, and a patch in the knee was sewn much better than I could have done it. I thanked the household for the exceptional night and headed off down the road back to town. From there it was a short hike back to the tent city we called our base and the tent I shared with 11 other men.

The Carolina maneuvers were a carbon copy of the Louisiana maneuvers. It was getting later in the fall and we were now getting frost in the mornings. Still Louisiana in the early fall warms up real well

On the way up from Louisiana the battalion march had been delayed and we did not reach our reconned staging site for the night. The Colonel decided it was time to go into camp for the night anyway and thought a big meadow alongside a river would be a fine encampment.

He ordered the battalion to make camp there. Several officers tried to change his mind but even my recon CO, Captain Waters, couldn't talk him out of it. A farmer came by with a piece of straw hanging out of his mouth and noticed all the large vehicles staging in the meadow for the night. I heard that conversation as well

"General, those heavy trucks and tractors are going to sink in the rain, this meadow floods." said the farmer in a slow southern drawl.

The Colonel had had enough second guessing of his decision and exploded on the poor farmer. "I am not a General I am a Colonel. I have personally walked this ground and it is more than suitable for our staging area."

"Yes sir," said the farmer "but when it rains it's gonna flood that meadow."

"I'll have you know sir that I have access to the finest metrological data and the best weather intelligence in the world. It will not rain."

With that prediction the Colonel had had enough conversation and left the farmer standing in the road.

I hung back and I saw the 11,000 pound wrecker sink deep as it rolled in to its assigned parking area. I sneaked my C&R car into some trees closer to the highway and out of sight. That night it rained and rained without stopping. It rained the next day and most of the next. Vehicles that tried to move sank in the mud, tanks and heavy trucks that did not move simply sank where they were parked

The entire Battalion was laying on its composite belly in the softened ground. As soon as work started everything in that meadow turned to horrible mud and ended that effort. I went to my Lieutenant and told him what I had done so he would have his transport. The Lieutenant said: "Case. God will bless you."

He let me get several cables hooked together and along with the crews of the lighter vehicles we were able to pull and winch some of the vehicles out of the mud to the hard ground. Often we would daisy chain two or more vehicles to pull out a vehicle stuck further in. But for all our efforts the mech elements of the battalion were stuck hard for a good week. Sometimes I still wonder what the army had to pay that farmer in damages for the destruction of his meadow.

It got to be near the middle of November 1941 and I was detailed with a Senior Grade Sergeant to go to some place north of us and meet another unit who would transfer some highly classified equipment to us. We had to be armed and loaded to accept the equipment. We were ordered not to stop anywhere along the road. Further we were not to surrender the equipment to anyone other than the assigned command communications officer.

We drove to the meeting and picked up the equipment and gassed up my C&R for the return trip. We were well on our way back to the outfit, it was after midnight with no moon and it was pitch dark. I caught a glimpse of car wheels spinning on a car that was upside down off to the left side of the road. I slammed on the brakes and backed to a spot alongside of the wreck. The Sergeant said: "Lord what do I do now? They will probably shoot both of us but we have to see what's down there."

He told me to take my gun. That was lucky because there were two boys and two girls in the wreck. Neither of the boys could walk so we got one on each side, with a kid sitting on my rifle and carried them to the C&R car. We got the two boys on top of the boxes in the back and the one girl who wasn't too badly hurt. We knew the second girl was in a bad way and was probably critical. She had bled a great deal before we got to her and I pulled my first aid kit from the C&R and bandaged her wound. I never knew what she hit.

We got her in the front seat so the Sergeant could hold her. I went very fast. We had some luck then because some cops saw us and chased us but I couldn't stop. I waved them up alongside us and hollered for them to lead us to the hospital. They did that and must have radioed ahead because several people were waiting at the hospital door.

The Sergeant was in a quandary again. The cops wanted us to go in and make the report. The Sergeant had a hard time making them understand he could not leave his cargo and that the equipment was highly classified material.

They finally left one officer with the Sergeant and the other went in with me. A nurse ran out into the lobby and asked everybody what their blood type was and I was the only odd type there. 'O' negative was required and that was on my dog tag. The Doc said I had to give blood or the kid would die. I lay on the table and made a live transfer. They left the hook-up in place and an hour later told me I had to donate again. This time he told me they had closed her up and if I would donate again it was a good chance that she would make it.

I had done the exact same procedure in Bradley Beach, New Jersey a little over a year before. That also was a teenaged girl from a car wreck and she had survived. All the radio stations had broadcast a plea for help. I was driving by and I heard the plea because I was driving a company car with a radio in it. I knew my blood type because I had recently donated to the blood bank so I pulled in and offered the blood.

Back in North Carolina, the Doc sent a note with us so the command would know we weren't out bar hopping and fooling around. The Sergeant and I had to sit through a board-of-inquiry which was rather quickly convened before the matter was settled. They had to verify that the equipment had not been compromised and that the classified nature of the items had been properly protected. After all that no one even said we had done the proper thing or congratulated us on doing a good deed.

At that time several of the one year men, who would not be needed on the trip home, were discharged from the service and shipped to their place of enlistment for separation. Late in November we rolled out and started for home. Even a rank amateur, as I was, could see the vast improvement in our march.

We were directed into the post through many different gates. We got into our Motor Pool about 22:00 hours and I thought how good my cot would feel. I was disappointed badly. We were not dismissed. Seems all the vehicles needed to be washed and cleaned and serviced. Tires needed changing, fuel tanks needed to be topped off, oil filters and lubricants had to be topped off and basically the unit could have moved out in just moments. Upon completion of the servicing of the vehicles we had to clean and store all organic weapons to the battalion, truck mounted machine guns, and then we got to clean our personal weapons rifles and pistols.

Any vehicle that could not be repaired on the spot had to be written up for parts and repairs needed and that paperwork had to be filed with the maintenance officer and his office. There was never the idea you could leave something undone until tomorrow. Once all that was accomplished you could return to the barracks where of course you needed to ensure you had a clean uniform and shined boots for tomorrow's formation. After that you could actually go to bed.

We had arrived on the post the night of December 6, 1941. All through the maneuvers I had been exempted from the extra duties roster because my job required me to be on standby 24 hours a day. I had to drive off on missions routine or urgent but I had to be ready at an instant's notice. The battalion First Sergeant (not the one that had stood up for me) hadn't forgotten me and my exemption from extra duties while in the field. He kept a book of soldiers that had made his list and my name was on top.

I got to bed somewhere around 02:30 am, the CQ got me up at 04:00 the same morning and informed me I was on KP. I walked over to the mess hall in a dazed exhaustion on Sunday morning of December 7, 1941 and that was how I started the war.

THE COMING OF WAR

07 December 1941 - 11 January 1943

The Mess Sergeant knew I had a radio so he told me if I would bring it into the mess hall, he would give me a good job. I jumped at that offer because I would be a DRO. (Dining Room Orderly). That's the best job a KP can get because all you do is bus tables for the officers and senior staff NCOs. We served breakfast without a hitch and the radio worked famously. Reception tended to fade due to atmospherics and needed constant adjustments. We were finishing cleanup from the Lunch detail when I couldn't get any music on the set.

I was fooling with the radio and reception was really lousy. The folks on mess duty wanted to hear some music, but the reception was badly garbled by excited and seemingly out of control broadcasters. We could not figure out what they were talking about but no matter what station I turned to I was getting the same nonsensical broadcast, something about battleships being sunk. Unfortunately it started to dawn on us that something very bad had happened and as we listen we heard the first reports of the bombing at Pearl Harbor.

The command reaction was immediate. Everyone was called off leave and those lounging in the barracks on a Sunday afternoon were called out into formation. Security was significantly tightened because although there was not yet a formal declaration we all knew the United States was now at war. Taxi drivers had been in the habit of whistling through the gate without stopping for the gate guard. On the first day of the war one did the same thing and a gate guard shot and killed him. Someone had evidently given the kid some wild instruction and the kid obeyed.

The Brass evidently wanted as many people as possible to start getting ready for later important duties. They assigned trainees every place they could find. One of the jobs was controlling people at the Bus Stop. Some guy who must have thought he was a tough guy broke into the front of the line to get on a bus headed for his home. The young kid trainee told him to go to the rear but the hard guy refused to do it and made tantalizing remarks to the kid. The trainee put up his rifle and shot the hard guy in the head. That resulted in a great furor and every soldier on the base was called into meetings and instructed in the proper handling of people.

So I guess it goes without saying that my last week of draftee service ended on that day. I recall I was washing my clothes and packing my things because I was to discharge the following Wednesday and would be on a train the next day. As hard as it was to accept that I was not going anywhere soon I guess I had it better than some of the other folks that discharged the week before. I understand that trains headed for home were stopped in mid-route and turned around to bring those soldiers back. Guys waiting for a plane were "escorted" by local sheriffs and police to the nearest train station and sent back to the bases from which they had just left.

I was the first of our draftees to be promoted to Corporal and that was quickly done after we arrived back at the post. I was made squad leader, Third Squad, Third Platoon, 'A' Company, 1st. Armored Division. This is where the story of my First Sergeant ends.

The Courts Martial found him guilty of misconduct in the presence of an officer, or something like that. He was busted to private and was assigned to my squad. That was a hard one to take. During the ensuing field work he taught us a lot. He never once complained about his court or the authorities who broke him. Months later when the 16th Engineers were establishing the beach head in North Africa he was restored to his rank of First Sergeant and I believe he retired at that rank.

Next in quick order I was assigned a brand new M3 Half Track with a 37 millimeter M3 towed cannon (yes both were named M3).

The M3 37mm cannon was the end of tank warfare - or so we had been told. When the 37mm cannon was designed, it was based off the German Pac36 gun which could penetrate any armor of its time. The M3 used armor piercing, high explosive, and anti-personnel called canister type of rounds. The armor piercing rounds were the ones that were so deadly to the tanks of 1934. Unfortunately by Sept 1939 the Nazi's showed that tank warfare was a long way from being obsolete. This is a clear case of the technology for the offense surpassing the abilities of the defense. As an anti-tank gun, the M3 was almost useless in Europe but did have some value in the Pacific with the lighter armor of the Japanese. It also proved a valuable weapon for mountain troops as it could be broken down and hauled up and down mountains.

To pull that gun we had a brand new White Motor Company M3 Scout Car – routinely called a half track. The vehicle was originally designed as an artillery tractor but proved so versatile it was used for just about everything, artillery hauling, troop transport, assault gun, antitank mount and logistics vehicle. It had seating for up to 13 men, 5 on each side in the back and three in the cab. Several configurations were made but ours mounted a 50 cal machine gun on a free swing pedestal mounted to the hull just above the cab of the vehicle. The vehicle was powered by a White 160x 386 cubic inch flat head 6 which produced 148 horse power.

The M3 weighed in at 15 tons and had an operational range of 175 miles with a top speed of 45mph on improved roads, cross country speed was roughly half of that and the vehicle made about 3 miles per gallon. We liked the vehicle; it was mechanically reliable and was relatively easy to maintain except for the rear support assembly which was a bear to pull. However once it got into combat it was labeled the Purple Heart Box, a grim reference to the medal awarded to folks that were wounded or killed in action. The armor plate was not effective against machineguns and the lack of overhead cover allowed artillery airbursts to wrack havoc on the embarked squads.

My gun was a long barrel rifle mounted on wheels. I had never seen one before and neither had any of my squad. The books on how to use the gun were not packaged with the gun and we didn't have those either. We were just told to go out to the range and see how to work it. We hooked the gun up to the halftrack and headed off to the firing range.

We gathered around it and opened a box that was on the gun's trailer. I had the men go through the cleaning procedure. As I recall the gun mount had spades and I had a working knowledge of that. We dug the gun in and leveled it. We all practiced operating the elevation mechanism, worked the breach and looked through the sighting scope.

We practiced all the functions of the weapon but I remember we didn't have any practice rounds and I was having misgivings about loading live rounds. One of the guys made the simple suggestion: have one guy hold his hands on the triggering device so nobody could get to it. We did that and we got away with it. We fooled with the gun for a couple of hours until everybody said they understood the operation.

We didn't break for lunch but went straight through for seven hours. Detachments were scattered all over the country side and getting food to them would be a major problem. I finally couldn't think of any more reasonable excuses for delaying the firing so I stood up and said: "I'll fire first because I'm the gun captain and if I blow up the cannon they can pull my stripes."

We had twelve men in the squad at that time and the box of rounds would allow each of us to fire two rounds. I said "we will each fire two rounds and then go in and see what the Lieutenant wants us to do next." We each fired our two rounds and after a while we started to hit stuff. The guys were excited about shooting the piece and shooting is so much more fun than cleaning.

The rounds were hard nose, and when they hit the old tanks that were set out as targets the anti-tank rounds would go through like it was made of tissue paper. The 37mm was very effective against World War 1 tanks – too bad we couldn't make the bad guys use only WW1 tanks. After firing we cleaned the gun, hooked it back to the halftrack and headed back to the ramp where we did a thorough cleaning of gun and halftrack and topped off the gas tanks and oil sumps.

When I reported to the Lieutenant he gave me a blank look and finally said:

"You mean you fired real rounds?"

"Yes Sir I thought you wanted us to familiarize ourselves with the gun"

"Yes but I didn't know you were going to shoot the thing. Everyone ok?"

"Yes Sir, no problem."

"Well ok then, mark it off on the training charts and secure for the day."

We never had to be told twice to secure for the day.

It wasn't long after that I was reassigned to conduct a class. This was a field problem. The Captain had a heavy machine gun placed on a knoll that was almost clear of cover on three sides and had a clear field of fire in the other direction. The problem was how to get the gun out of there. Heavy guns usually have riflemen positioned to cover them and protect them until the gun can be turned to direct fire on any new threat. That is about what was set up here. Only one approach was possible.

We had to come up a narrow gulch and use the cover of the ragged sides to gain position for a rifle attack. There was a stream in the gulch and any attackers had to wade in it part of the time. It was February and it was cold.

While my classes only had to get in the water once, I had two classes a day every day of the work week and it wasn't long before I had double Pneumonia and Pleurisy. Shortly thereafter I added Shingles to the list. Needless to say I spent some time in the hospital.

Back when we were in the Louisiana maneuvers the army was getting nervous about the possibility of having to fight in the Pacific. The way we understood it they would administer the Yellow Fever shot to the entire army on a certain date. They set it up and did it as far as we knew. Much of the stuff they injected was bad and an immense number of soldiers went down with yellow fever. I believe the figure released to us was 140,000.

I got my shot and was walking up a path through the jungle and men were collapsing along the way. I didn't but the yellow fever disaster almost killed me anyway. The hospitals didn't have enough people to handle the yellow fever load, they sure didn't have enough room for sickies

Many hospitals were filled beyond capacity. Both Army and Civilian as the Army medical system was swamped by the yellow fever disaster. Civilian hospitals took up the overflow and clinics and Churches were used as well. It was into that situation I was sent with my problems. Hospitals were struggling but didn't have people to fill the need. I was driven to the hospital in a truck and let off at the front door. I was terribly sick but asked a fellow where to go. He simply said you'll have to wait a while all the nurses and Doctors are having their coffee.

By that time I was helpless and I fell down beside a butt can vomiting into that. A man knelt down beside me and asked me what was wrong.

"I can't get up I'm sick." I was crying and couldn't control it. I felt stupid.

He said: "you sure are sick." He had put his hand on my forehead. "Let me help you sit against the wall for just a minute."

He got up and ran to a door a few yards down the hall and must have burst in there. I could hear some of what he was screaming at the people in there. "You have a man laying in his own vomit in the hall with at least a hundred and six fever and you are sitting here making jokes."

I have never seen, or heard, a full bird Colonel go off on officers and ladies like that. He was furious and nearly out of control. He used some words that I'll bet those ladies never heard before. Turns out I later found that this Colonel had just been assigned as the CO of that hospital and that was his first experience with his new command. Don't think there were a lot of coffee breaks on the schedule after that incident.

A stretcher appeared quickly and after I was put on it I don't remember anymore. I was either unconscious or sedated for the next ten days, I was told. The Doctor who signed me out later told me that one of the nurses had watched over me during her time off duty. She washed me with alcohol, moved me in bed to make me rest better, and many more of those little cares. The Doctor said without her I would certainly have died. The load of the yellow fever guys was more than they could handle. All hospitals were in the same fix so they couldn't get help. I tried to find the lady to thank her but couldn't. I asked the doctor to do it for me.

They sent me back to the company to make room for someone else. In a couple of weeks I was back on my feet and then the big event happened. A letter arrived, addressed to me, from the Commanding General, V Corps.

The mail clerk took that to the First Sergeant who took it to the Company Commander. The Captain called me in his office and told me to read the letter. If it was a personal thing I was to keep it to myself. If it had anything to do with the command I was to reveal the contents.

He had me sit down in his office and read the letter while he took a stroll to the water dispenser. The letter simply said they had record that I had applied for the Air Corps in 1934 and if I was still interested this letter constituted authority for me to go to Bowman Field to take the aptitude test. My Company Commander was to provide the transportation.

I didn't think of it at the time but eventually it hit me. This is the pre- computer days they didn't even have the artillery flight computer designed yet and this meant that some secretary, probably some aged little old bitty had read my letter, filed it, and then nearly 8 years later found my application. That was some phenomenal records keeping, and it was all done by hand.

I showed the letter to the Captain and all of the sudden things started happening in a hurry - a very big hurry. My Captain tried to talk me out of going – I was the first Corporal of the 41 Draft, I had my own gun crew and there was strong possibility of me being the first Sergeant of the 41 Draft but that was a futile try compared with the opportunity to fly.

I showed up at the air field and reported to the auditorium. Corporals taking the test were definitely in the minority there. The test was a color in the dot test that was machine read. The test was easy for me consisting of practical problem solutions, the Bible, and deductions. I scored highest in an auditorium full of about five hundred men including officers and college men. We were told to stand by after the test and await the results of the scoring.

A Major was in charge of the test and had the scores for the class.

He had me stand in recognition of my high score and said "Corporal Case. You will go far in this Army." I'm sure what he really meant was go many miles, which I surely did.

I had aced the test, was fully recovered from my illness so the physical was breeze, and I had better than 20/20 vision so I owned the sight and color tests. I had only one problem to overcome before I could go to pilot training. That was my teeth. The Air Corps was finicky about that – I could get by with my teeth in the Army but the Air Corps wanted perfect teeth. (I guess for all those photo ops with Hollywood starlets while making movies.) I was set up to have some dental work done and was assigned to one of the assistants.

This man had graduated from medical school early because the Army figured he could do many of the lesser jobs. When he got to the hospital he was just an "in turn" (intern) which meant he did anything that came along when it came along.

He took one look in my mouth and said: "man you got two teeth that have to come out." I told him I had to have those teeth to gain admission to the Air Corps. He said "I can't help that. I can't fix them." I didn't know enough in those days to say I wanted another opinion. I just thought I had to accept the treatment.

I had a peculiar characteristic in my molars. The inside roots all had a very strong hook under the bone and had to be broken in order to remove the two teeth. The dental assistant set up and was struggling but couldn't get the tooth out. He finally went to an office across the hall and got another man to assist. They talked for a couple of minutes and the new man wanted to try something. The first man got a solid head lock on me and the second man was going to try and break the root by standing on the chair and pulling the tooth with the pliers. It literally looked like something you'd see in a three stooges film.

About that time a real dentist walked past and saw the unusual arrangement. He came in and said

"Hold up here. What's going on?" He bent over and said to me "how's it going? Are you hurting?"

I told him "that part isn't too bad, those men have given me four shots of Novocain I'm not feeling much of anything."

He shook his head and told me to open up so he could have a look.

He mopped out my mouth and I said: "I asked them not to pull the teeth because I had to have them to get into the Air Corps but they said they had to come out."

The dentist was a Light Bird – a Lieutenant Colonel and he turned to the two who were standing by. "You two are dismissed. See me in my office in one hour, and don't be late."

I know in retrospect, I was doped up pretty good, but I didn't miss the tone of the last remark. Despite the fog in my brain from all the drugs I was very happy not have to keep that appointment.

He said to me "Son I'm going to handle the rest of this. If they haven't broken the bone I'll get you in the Air Corps."

In the days that followed he filled the two molars with concrete. Those two teeth stayed with me for many, many years and got me in the Air Corps. With a clean dental record that was the last hurdle and I became a Cadet.

Leaving the company was a kind of a sad feeling. I was surprised because up to then all I wanted to do was get out of the Army. I had said: "if we actually go into combat I will enlist in the Navy anyway. All my family had been navy and both of my elder brothers were in the Navy at that time. I still wasn't that clear on how the Army worked. Inter-service transfers were possible but extremely rare.

I was loaded into a railroad car of ancient vintage and sent to Santa Ana, California. I was stunned. There were trains unloading all around the area that I could see. Later when we started our classes we were told there were 90,000 Cadets on that base.

Life on the base was physical training first and classes of all sorts second. Mass calisthenics went on without ceasing. We had to learn to march again because there was no distinction between those men that had come directly from the civilian world and those like me that had already done this stuff. After we had the basic stuff again we started training in our specific field; pilots here, communications types there, navigators there, etc. There were 90,000 but we were not all pilots.

One class that was impossible for me was reading and sending code. Not one time did I get that right but evidently there must have been a lot of people just like me because they passed me through. All other subjects were easy for me but one.

31

An interesting event took place during that time. A Jap submarine came close to the beach and fired several shells into an oil field. That upset the brass and they decided a detachment of cadets would be armed and sent to the beach each evening to help repel any attempt by the Japs to land on our coast. I was in that comedy.

We were armed with some unheard of Enfield rifles probably from the Boer War. We would load the guns in a tent before getting out on the road. We would chamber the round prior to engaging the safety lock. That was the way those old guns were rigged. A lot of the guns would go off and we could see the stars through the roof of that tent. We eventually went to patrol with ammunition in our pocket and an empty rifle on our shoulder.

We would march out 7 miles to the beach and march back each morning and then go to classes. Standing watch 4 hours of the night and then sleeping in the sand all night and marching 14 miles a day on top of the daily exercise requirement made us very attentive to the classes being given in the hot wooden sheds where we studied to be pilots. Naturally instructors were so sympathetic to our plight. It was routine to see Cadets falling off the benches on the floor totally passed out from lack of sleep. Others had the cadet bump, a bruise on the middle of your forehead where they had fallen asleep and bashed their head on the hard wooden table. Those that dozed off got the entire platoon doing pushups and jumping jacks.

I think we only stayed two months at Santa Ana. During that time several things happened to me that have lasted all my life. In the army when people are assigned to something names are often taken from a roster. Most rosters are in alphabetical order. That system prevailed at Santa Ana. When we were assigned to tents on arrival at the base my tent was down the line a bit. My last name started with 'C' and all the men in that tent were 'Cs' I never got to know any of those fellows because their schedules were different than mine. Their names are long since forgotten.

However a few tents down was a man named Carol a different last name than the other men in that tent. How he got in there I don't know. He and I had many associations during our stay there. Just a few more tents down was another man named Dan David from Pueblo

Colorado. He and I had many adventures and I will have much to say about him.

Carol's dad was a General so the Army was rather careful with him. We did class work together and in PT we stayed close. By the middle of the stay we were friends. One day he came into my tent. He said 'I just heard we are getting a weekend pass the week before we leave here. My intended is going to the University in Louisiana and before she goes I want to take her dancing.

I thought 'ok so what does this have to do with me?' I figured Carol had the watch the night of the dance and needed me to take his shift. I had nothing else to do so was getting ready to say yes I'll take your watch when Carol dropped the bombshell, "She has a real nice friend and she wants me to get her a date so we can go together. How about it will you join us?'

I told him I was a hick and never had so much as walked down a street with a girl other than my baby sister. I wouldn't be anything but a drag. Why not get one of the guys who can entertain the girl?

Carol was firm. "No. I want you to come. We'll have a nice time. She is nice and you will be at ease with her."

I finally agreed and it turned into a pleasant evening but I couldn't say I was at ease. We picked the girls up at their sorority house and that was a very posh place. I had never been in a house like that in my life. When they came down the wide carpeted stairs I wanted to run, they were wearing beautiful flowing gowns the likes of which I had never seen before except in the movies.

We took the girls to the Palladium where Lawrence Welk's big band was playing. The place was alive with actors and stars. Gary Cooper and his wife were chaperoning Shirley Temple and Jane Withers. They stood beside us much of the time and our dates had regular conversation with all of them. Later when we took the girls back to their house my date asked me if I thought I would be able to come back again. I didn't know.

Later when I was in combat she wrote me several letters. I looked forward to getting them. Then I got one from Carol's (now wife) telling me the girl had died. A sudden attack of acute appendicitis and they couldn't get her to the hospital in time.

One Sunday I was sitting in my tent and a Lieutenant poked his head in. He said "Fall out Mister." I grabbed my hat and hurried out into the street. Several cadets were already out there. I saw Dan David and stopped beside him. I asked what's going on but he shrugged his shoulders and told me the officers are grabbing everybody they could find in the tents. There weren't many it being Sunday and all the cadets with any sense had already left the base.

A Captain came out and looked us over. He picked out four of us and it was obvious he picked guys about the same size that had matching clothing. He told us to jump in a truck that was standing there so Dan and I climbed in. He said we were going to town to a radio station to see what they wanted.

The first guy I ran into at the radio station was Tom Harmon, the famous all American football player from the University of Michigan. He won the Heisman trophy his senior year and led the nation in scoring in 1939 and 1940. He was a second Lieutenant and all gussied up in his new uniform. There was one of the starlets that they used for these events who was a real looker. I don't know what was wrong with Harmon. Every time that girl came near him he would get all red faced and flustered. I thought "I never thought I'd see anybody worse than me."

What the occasion was all about was they were going to introduce the Army Air Forces Song and they wanted Army Air Forces people to sing it. I'm sure everybody has heard it – "off we go into the wild blue yonder". The band played it once or twice for us so we could hear the tune and then we ran through it a couple of times reading from the sheet music. And then it was time to go on the air. It was undoubtedly the roughest treatment the song ever received but that is how I got on national radio. I never did get a singing contract or record deal out of it.

A couple of days later the Army sponsored an evening when Eddy Cantor brought his show to the base. The great star Dinah Shore was the main attraction for certain although there were other great acts as well. She was quite young at that time and was quite a looker. I hadn't heard about the show and Dan David stopped on his way to the stage to get me to go. As I said before there were 90,000 guys on the base and I'm quite sure every one of them was at the show. It was outdoors in a boxing ring with huge speakers all over the place.

The Eddy Cantor show was the biggest network program in existence at that time. Some guy had written a song that, for the time, was considered somewhat risqué. Dinah had been singing it during the regular network program and the censors cut it off in the middle. That raised a furor all over the world. Well; when the girl got up to sing here, that mob of guys began screaming for the song. The name was 'I Said No' and the part that was a bit racy went like this:

I said "No!" he said "Why?"
I said "No!" he said "Why?"
I said "No!" he said "Try?"
I said "Maybe."

He said "Now?" I said "Well"
He said "Ah this is swell."
"And you will never know how much it will mean."
"So at last confess"
I said "Yes, Yes, Yes, Yes, Yes!"
That's how I subscribed to Liberty Magazine

Dinah tried to sing the song she was scheduled to sing but the guys wouldn't let her. She finally went and sat down.

Cantor didn't know what to do. There wouldn't be any more show if she didn't sing that was for sure. He finally went to her and they had some argument. Shortly Dinah went to the mike and the crowd quieted. The band struck the introduction. She sang a line or so when some kook let go a big whistle and that set off a lot of catcalls and Dinah started to cry. Now Dan started to laugh as he thought the entire affair was the funniest thing he ever heard of.

The Military Police took Miss Shore out the back way and secluded her someplace. The show was over because the men left by the thousands. It strikes me as funny after all these years; all those thousands came only to see/hear Dinah sing that song. They weren't interested in the jokes or the dancers or anything else in what was a great program.

Dan David reacted differently than anyone else there. He laughed 'til I thought he would be sick. Everyone would know Dan David later as Dan Rowan of the Rowan and Martin TV show. For years they were the biggest comedy show on TV.

Shortly after the show our assignments were posted on bulletin boards all over the base. All the guys in my tent were betting that I would get Bomber or Navigator school because of my age. I had requested Single Engine Pilot School but that was a tough school to get into. I had already logged almost 70 hours in light planes from my civilian days and I'm sure that swung the decision in my favor.

My assignment was King City, California. I was a very happy man but it wasn't over yet. They would try once more to get me out of the pilot program. The philosophy in those days was that anyone over 25 years old was too old to fly fighters. They certainly didn't know how wrong they were.

The equipment at King City was Ryan low wing trainers (all metal). My instructor was a crop duster pilot and he knew the instant we got in the plane I had previous time. He later told me that, as I was leaving he didn't know if I had more time than he did. I had to laugh at that because he had a couple of thousand hours.

The Ryan PT 22 Primary Trainer was built by the same manufacturer that built Lucky Lindberg's Spirit of St Louis. It was basically a kite with a lawn mower engine and was used to weed out those folks that had zero flying aptitude and teach the fundamentals to those folks that might have some prospect of flying.

The PT-22 was called the Recruit and was a two-seater, instructor and cadet. The plane had a Kinner motor that deliver 160 hp for a normal cruising speed of 100mph with a range of 231 miles. No one ever flew 231 miles in the plane but it could make several hops on one tank of gas. The Recruit was a forgiving plane with a stall speed at roughly 55mph, fixed landing gear, and 14 pound wing loading.

The plane had adjustable flaps and wing trim controls so the very basics of flying could be accomplished. Once those were mastered the cadets were given the opportunity to fly solo – one take off, one orbit about the field, and one landing. If all that was accomplished the cadet was funneled off to the basic trainer.

My next stop was Chico, California. This was the basic training school under the command of Colonel John Nissley. I was assigned to M flight Class 43A along with 46 other cadets. We had Captain Anderson as Flight Commander and Lieutenant Alexander as the Assistant Flight Commander. There were 8 Second Lieutenant Flight Instructors most of them very good at training cadet pilots. There were four flights so we were training roughly 200 cadets. We had aircraft called BT-13 s and I was starting to get into heavier and more powerful planes. It wasn't much on performance but we got some feel for the bigger ships.

The Vultee BT 13 Valiant had a 450 HP nine cylinder engine with a speed of 180mph and a range of 725 miles. It had radios, landing flaps, more advanced trim, and an adjustable variable pitch propeller. It required more skill to fly than the Recruit but was significantly more advanced. We practiced formation flying, primary stunts like hammer heads and loops and cross country navigation. We also learned to fly and land at night, night navigation was a real task and landing on instruments and landing lights was a real shocker the first time I tried it. I do recall that when we had night flying we always had glazed and frosted donuts and a glass of Lemonade. Why they didn't give us coffee for the late night flights I never understood.

The crew was still two men, the instructor and the trainer but the trainer took control of the aircraft more frequently. The intermediate craft was designed to get the student comfortable with more complex aircraft and better equipment before moving them off to advanced flight school.

Again all the classes came easy for me except for that horrid box on swivel call the Link Training Device. Link training was a hateful thing for me and I don't know how I passed that. Link trainers were "flight simulators" built by a guy named Ed Link who was a former organ builder. That is how the story goes; personally I think Satan designed the thing.

The trainer would react to the pilot's motions and actions and actually was a safe way to train people how to fly a plane. The absolute worst training evolution was the Link trainer covered in a hood to simulate flying on instruments alone. It was hot, it was muggy inside the canopy, and there was nothing to visually orient on except the gages and dials, which often caused folks to get nauseous and vomit in the trainer. No matter how hard you clean that you just cannot get rid of the smell.

Now more trouble started for me. My instructor was a nice little guy who basically all he wanted to do was teach me to fly. He had several successes and he was switched to another flight that was struggling. The replacement instructor was a junior trainer and he right away started on the age thing, asking me how they let me into the program in the beginning. He looked at my Preference Statement and said "Mister I can't approve your request for Pursuit. You're way too old." he said yet he hadn't even flown with me.

I followed my administrative chain of command and requested to see my Lieutenant to request a review of the situation. I went to an Army pilot and he said he would see a 1st Lieutenant who had all the say in those matters.

However it went over a different route. The base commander, Colonel Nissley, called me in his office where my Flight Commander Captain Anderson had previously briefed him on my performance. The Colonel asked me why I wanted Pursuit. I said all my life I wanted to fly the little Pursuit planes. Single engine seemed to be what I wanted. Multi-engine with a crew didn't seem right for me. "Sir every one up the line has approved me."

He thought for some time before he told me he would send me up with the ranking Lieutenant and if I got by him he would approve my request. I didn't sleep much that night.

I was waiting at the plane when he walked out. He stood looking at me. I didn't know what to do but the Lieutenant didn't seem much interested in the test. I said: "Sir is there anything you want me to do?"

He said "Mister this is your flight so let's get on with it."

I took the bit in my teeth – it was clear nobody was going to help me with anything and that I would just have to put on a great performance. I did the walk around inspection and then asked him to get aboard. He did and I called all clear to the crew chief. He signaled for 'Start Engine' and I went through the procedure for a cold engine start.

I ran down the checklist on my knee board, pulled the paper to the back of the board and signaled the ground crew I was ready to start engine. To start those engines, one had to place a crank in the engine and two men, one on each side of the crank, would wind up a gyro until it reached phenomenal speeds. The pilot would engage the gyro and it would turn the engine over. The ground crew did that and when the instruments were in order I signaled to pull chocks and then rolled out.

I called the tower for taxi instructions and got to the takeoff position. I ran the engine up and checked the Mags. There was no runway at Chico it was a huge square mat and planes took off at any and all orientation to the control tower. When I throttled back to idle I called the tower for takeoff instructions. I also reported the flight was local, duration one hour. They called back and gave me 'clear for takeoff' and I followed standard procedure for that field.

I taxied to the launch area, pointing the nose of the BT 13 in the direction of takeoff. I adjusted the variable pitch prop for takeoff, applied power, and released the brakes. I started rolling down my section of the square and built up ground speed. The BT's tail came up and I held the plane on the ground getting that last bit of speed before pulling up into the air. As soon as I had flight speed I retracted my wheels and pulled in my flaps, basically executing a perfect takeoff.

I climbed out to 3,000 feet and went through all the preliminary turns and stalls. I was a bit hesitant with the complete lack of instruction or detail but I knew the evaluator wasn't going to help me with instructions so I started my acrobatics. I knew I could do more than most basic students. I did loops and rolls and then snap rolls, a hammerhead, and an outside stall. I might be kicked out of the flight school at the end of this hop so I thought I'd enjoy possibly my last flight in the Army.

At that he called and said: "OK. Let's go home." I thought everything had gone well and was feeling good. About 600 feet altitude on the way in the engine went to idle. The Lieutenant had chopped the throttle from the rear cockpit to see how I would handle an "emergency" situation. I hadn't even thought about a forced landing. I was caught cold. Students were always supposed to have a field in mind for situations exactly as I was facing now. I was low and didn't have much time. I lined on the first thing I saw - a skinny pasture along a river overgrown with tall weeds. It didn't look like much but it did look like I could put the BT in there, getting it back out was a problem for another time.

I kept gliding down and it was apparent the instructor was going to let me land. I knew my procedure had been right and my use of flaps that had put me down in the first part of the field had been right. The landing gear was dropped starting to drag through the tops of the weeds and I was starting to round out for touch down. Just as I was about to flair for final he eased on the throttle and I got power. I took control of the throttle and applied full power to get my speed and pulled up to cruising altitude. He said head for the barn and I lined up on the landing pad. I was rattled and thought I might goof the landing but luck stayed and I made a good three point landing.

We got out and the Lieutenant stood by while I filled out the post flight form. He took that and was studying it. I was still nervous from the dead stick landing procedure so I said: "I guess I didn't pick a very good field for the forced landing." He looked up and said "you would have made it wouldn't you?"

I answered: "yes Sir we were in the field OK."

The Lieutenant initialed the form and handed it to the crew chief and just walked off. I didn't know what else to do so I went back to the barracks and started packing like the other guys were doing.

The next morning the Assignment Sheets were on our bulletin board and there was Case on top of the sheet and assigned to Luke Field - Advanced Training, Single Engine.

The Cadets were offered an option. We could take government transportation or take the money and go on our own. I took the money and hitch hiked. I caught a couple of rides and then was picked up by a grandfather type driving a rickety old truck. He told me he and his two brothers were in World War One.

During his rambling he told me his family was in the gold mining business. The rest of his family was all dead now and beside his mining operations he owned eleven Beauty Parlors. He was a seedy looking person so I thought he was putting me on but, of course, didn't say anything.

He told me one other thing. "When me and my brothers got ready to leave for the war my mother was quite upset. Then she handed each of us a little piece of paper that was folded around something. They was 'gold nuggets.' She told us not to lose them and they would bring us luck so we would come back home. We all did."

About that time we were coming to the top of the big hill at Bakersfield. I don't know what is there now but at that time it was a barren place. The old man pulled over and said: "I want to stop for a minute." I thought he was making a relief stop.

I saw he was throwing back the corner of the canvas which covered his truck box. He refastened the canvas and got back in the cab. He had a mason jar half full of gold nuggets. He poured some out in his hand and picked out a flat one about a half inch long and a quarter of an inch wide.

He gave it to me and said: "my mother was one of those Saints. She gave us boys a nugget to keep us safe and make us think of her. I'm going to do what she did and I hope you will come home."

I carried that nugget in my wallet for 50 years before I lost it.

I got to Luke on November 12, 1942. It was hotter than anything I had ever experienced before. The commander there was a full Colonel. He was said to be the youngest Full Bird in the army. It was also said he was 26 years old. I never figured out how that was possible but that was the situation when I got there.

That guy had issued orders that all Cadets would run at all times starting when a Cadet left a building and continuing until he reached another building. He also ordered all Cadets to wear full Garrison uniforms which included jackets and neckties. One more order was that when Cadets were in formations they would always be at attention.

That situation had evidently been enforced all through the summer and early fall. It was impossible to believe anyone could do such a thing. The temperatures were cool in the 90s but in the summer it was in the100s and routinely broke 105. Someone with connections evidently got to his congressman and about three days after we got there it came to a screeching halt. The inspectors relieved the Colonel instantly. All the Cadets he had washed out because they fainted in the heat, while standing for long periods in garrison uniforms, were called back. The government had spent a great deal of money to get those men that far into the program and it was ridiculously stupid to flunk pilots simply because they hailed from Northern states and were not used to the heat.

That Colonel was sent to Gila Bend where it was even hotter than Phoenix if that is possible, and there were only tents to live in. He eventually was sent to Ondonga in the Solomons and I never heard of him again.

Besides our class there was a class of Chinese going through and checking out in P-36s. The Chinese were experience pilots but the equipment they had flown was somewhat primitive. They had a bunch of the old P36 that the French had left in Asia. It makes sense that the Chinese would use them when they got back. The Chinese students had a deal of trouble with the planes and quickly wiped out some of them

One student was brought before a board to see if the cause could be found. After a rather futile effort to communicate with the student as to why they kept crashing the planes the board tried one last time.

"Why didn't you do what the tower told you to do?"

The student, in desperation, said: "too many red lights and horns and bells. I could not hear the tower."

"Those are the safety devices to warn you of a poor approach."

The student replied "too much noise to hear tower."

Basically the safety devices were too advanced for the pilots. I heard they removed the warning lights for most of the systems and the Chinese pilots' performance dramatically improved.

I went through most of the courses with little to no trouble. Instrument flying was a perplexing problem for me and I soon got worried that I'd be left back to repeat that with the next class. That problem involved flying blind, finding the beam, orienting yourself in order hit the Marker and then the Cone.

It was nearing the end of my class and I still hadn't passed the flight on finding the beam and homing to the cone. My instructor was a fine man who worked hard to get his students qualified. He gave me an extra hour on my beam problem but I still couldn't hit it.

His name was Gore and he was way over due for promotion. He was a First Lieutenant at Luke and nearly a year later I saw him in the Philippines and he was still a First Lieutenant. I always wondered what had happened to him. He had tried so hard to get me through the school.

When he couldn't put it off any longer Gore set me up a flight with a kid just out of flying school. When I met the kid I knew he didn't know any more about markers and cones than I did. I'm sure Gore did that on purpose.

We got off and I climbed to the specified altitude and he told me to get under the hood He made a couple of quick turns and wobbled the stick a couple of times. That was supposed to disorient me.

Then he said: "Ok. It's all yours." I tuned to the proper frequency with no trouble and using the compass swung to the west and just sat still until suddenly I heard the signal (a code letter) telling me I was east of the beam. I was overjoyed at that piece of luck. Now I didn't know whether I was inside the marker or outside the marker. That's where I got baffled. It doesn't seem difficult now but then I was so nervous everything seemed difficult. What do I do now? I kept flying and suddenly I was in the beam. I went on through and when I got the other quadrant signal I flew for one minute and tried to decide if I should turn left or right. I was getting more rattled every second.

In desperation I just swung left using the compass. A couple of seconds later I hit the cone dead center. I hadn't the faintest idea where I was in relation to the cone when I started that turn.

The kid in the back said, "Let's go home" and I was through.

My class was said to be the biggest class ever to go through. On January 2, 1943 we were graduated and on January 3, 1943 we were commissioned Second Lieutenants and presented our wings. One other event at that time was that FDR asked Congress for 100 billion dollars for the war effort. I remember reading that in the local newspapers and thinking to myself there could be no greater sum. I also thought that with that kind of money being invested we were real serious about winning the war.

Everyone was sent home for thirty days. I assumed the government wanted everyone to see their families and the families would have some time with us, because the next step would be to prepare for and go to the combat theaters all over the world.

My old outfit, the 1st Armored Div. had been sent to Ireland for staging. They were being prepared for the North Africa landing Operation Torch. Torch started on 8 November 1942, and finished on 11 November. In an attempt to pincer Axis forces, Allied forces (American and British), landed in Vichy-held French North Africa where it was assumed that there would be little to no resistance. Since the Nazis held the Vichy French forces relatives at gun point they put up a strong and bloody resistance and my old unit lost heavily. The engineers had to establish the beachhead and they suffered devastating losses, they lost over 35% and were considered combat ineffective because of the mauling the French gave our guys. Even now I thank God for saving me from that trial.

My 30 day leave was a wonderful slow time. I slept until I woke up naturally every day, naturally meaning not to awaken as a result from the crash of a canon or some troop leader blowing a whistle or beating a bell. I used my brother-law's-car but to this day never thought to ask about my little Pontiac. If I did I can't recall it.

When the leave was over I got on a train to St. Petersburg, Florida. Only a few days later I was shipped across the bay to Pinellas. That was a wonderful break because that outfit had brand new P-40Fs. That was one of the great thrills of my life. The training command had gotten the P40Fs because the Brits had refused them but they were the hottest machine I had ever flown.

The F model had British Rolls Royce Engines in them. That engine had a two stage blower and that plane would haul. I distinctly remember thinking that if the training command had planes this good how much better the front line equipment must be. I was still working on that how the Army works thing. I'm not sure I ever figured it out. I would not see anything so good again for a long time and never in combat.

We got about 25 hours of advanced flight training. As part of our flying time we would fly over the Bay. Straight across from us was MacDill Army Airfield and they were checking out air crews in Martin B-26 Marauders. That airplane was referred to as 'clipped wing 26s'. The airplane proved very dangerous for low skilled junior Bird Men and even advanced pilots had difficulties with them.

As we flew over the bay we could see the bottom easily because it wasn't deep. There were numerous B-26s laying down there. The kids coined a catchy cliché: 'One a day in Tampa Bay'.

When I was a private at Fort Knox the army was using many young pilots to ferry the Clip Wings around the country from the factory. Many were scheduled into Bowman field in Louisville for servicing.

It was a bad judgment on the part of the Brass. Bowman field was the worst arrangement I ever encountered in the United States particularly for high performance aircraft. It was too short, had telephone poles and wires just outside the fence, and the strip was high on both ends with a deep depression in the center.

The effect of that was if you didn't know the field, you'd come in and as you tried to round out to set down; the field would drop away and the bird would float down over the depression in the middle. High performance aircraft eat up ground quickly. Since your wheels aren't on the ground you can't use brakes.

The worst possible B-26 accidents occurred when those kids would try to throttle up and go around. In several cases they weren't good enough and they smashed into pretty much everything in the general area.

We at Fort Knox heard of the accidents several times. The paradox was that at Fort Knox we had Goodman Field which was flat as a table and long as a highway. Why the Brass didn't schedule the B-26s in there was beyond us. It was only 35 miles further which is about 4 minutes in a B-26.

The airplane's reputation got so bad that Colonel Doolittle made a tour in one demonstrating what the aircraft could do if properly handled. He did well with the demonstration but he left out the part where he showed what happens when the bird is loaded with a ton of bombs and loses an engine on take-off. It was not well publicized but one of the engines failing on takeoff was a common occurrence. The cockpit was overly complex - the dash board was a maze of instruments and controls and levers on the side walls and floor. It was not well laid out and a pilot needed a lot time in the ship before ever trying to take to the skies.

I made up my mind if I ever had to fly one of the B26s and had a failure close to the ground I would chop the other engine when the bird started to roll and go straight in. Of course if you have space below you, you can trim up and have a lot more options. Still the reputation of the B-26 was that of widow maker. The Marauder had to be flown at exact airspeeds, the 150 mph landing speed was intimidating to pilots who were used to much slower speeds, and whenever they slowed down below manufacture's specs, the aircraft would stall and fall out of the sky, at low altitudes that was called a crash

One night they called all the fighter pilots at MacDill into the mess hall at midnight. There were about 50 of us standing around in our shorts and t shirts in what was a very strange uniform for the formation, but we were told to come as we were and midnight other than the duty officer was sleep uniform. The Major got right to the point.

"Guys we got a sudden assessment to ship out some pilots. We hope we will get enough volunteers to fill the quota. If not we will have to appoint enough to fill the quota."

I was standing next to a friend with whom I had gone through the entire training cycle. James 'Hap' Chandler was a southern boy out of Arkansas who was quiet but when he spoke – people listened. He was a handsome man and I imagine many a lady would have liked an introduction but he was somewhat shy as well. He leaned over and said "Come on Case, let's go – We'll get back sooner."

Hard to fight that kind of logic. He put his hand up, so I did too. Dan David also volunteered as did probably 10 more. We didn't know if we were slated to the Pacific or European theaters, we were just going to go. Later one of the P-40 guys who was with Chandler in New Guinea said he went down in flames. He didn't bail out so the guy figured he had been hit.

We went back to the barracks got dressed and packed up. They gave us breakfast and then trucked us down to the flight line. We were loaded onto a DC-3, a commercial airliner that was being "used" by the government for a bit. That got us to the Carolinas but was grounded there with a maintenance problem. We made out as best we could in an old hanger.

The next morning they loaded us into a DC-2 which was the predecessor to the Douglas DC3. The DC-2 went into production in 1934 and was a good aircraft, fairly new but it was not the DC-3. It looked very similar to the 3 in that they both had the low wing and aerodynamically smooth features, rounded nose and graceful fuselage, but the DC-2 had two Wright GR 1820 9-cylinder engines rated at 730hp and a gross weight of 18,500 pounds which was approximately 6000lbs of cargo. The DC-3 had either the Wright cyclone 1,100hp engines or the later versions with the Pratt and Whitney 14 cylinder radial engines producing 1,200hp. It came in at 25,000lbs with a cargo capacity of just over 9,000lbs.

Our DC-2 was a very old transport probably one of the first in the production line and wasn't supposed to carry as many passengers as the DC-3 which had many more seats and a lot more horse power. It must have been the only thing they could find during the night, and we were a priority transport. I believe they did not top off the tanks in an effort to reduce the takeoff weight, because all 13 pilots were put on that old bird.

The flight was scheduled to New York so we kind of thought 'look out Hitler we are coming'. The aircrew was civilians under contract to the government to ferry supplies and replacements around to "non-combat" areas. Our pilot must have known what he was doing because after we were loaded and a couple of guys were sitting on the floor he started up and moved to the end of the field where he taxied out into the farthest edge of the approach area. His props were cutting scrub and blowing dirt back in great clouds. He got every inch of room on that strip that he could. When I realized what he was doing, added to the knowledge that the old ship only had small engines, I would have given a month's pay to get off.

The guy ran up his engines as hard as they would go and I saw him literally standing on the brakes. He let the engines howl before releasing the brakes and the plane leapt forward upon release jerking the passengers back into their seats, the folks on the deck having no hand holds simply rolled backwards. Despite the powerful release, we really were not going very fast. He rolled out taking up the entire strip before the tail came up. It seemed to me like he would never get the tail off the ground but he did.

Our man never got the aircraft off the ground while he was on the runway. He rolled straight off the end and started down a gentle slope sinking toward the trees. He was gaining speed but that was agonizingly slow. The rough ground actually helped as we bounced a bit, gained speed, settled back on the ground, and bounced again a bit higher. The ship slowly rose into the air and he pulled in his landing gear as quickly as possible. We could not have been more than 10 feet off the ground and were skimming the scrub bushes as we clawed for altitude. He leveled out just over the trees to our front and barely cleared them as well. We felt we could kill everyone connected with that takeoff.

While we were in the air we were diverted to Knoxville where we were joined by a second transport plane. We both lined up on the strip and the other plane landed first and we followed immediately behind. We touched down and looked at the lead plane as it hit the corner of a hanger and exploded. We never knew why that happened but we all saw it. It was absolutely the worse transport flight I had ever had, but the war was young and there are more transport stories.

We were met by trucks and taken to an airline DC-3. This one was all new and shiny and even better, this one included a lovely young hostess. The guys crowded around her until the pilot came back and said we had to spread out or spin in. It was a tough decision but we all went back to our seats. The girl was a quiet, pleasant person who served us Coca Colas. We made up some of the lost sleep of the previous night. The lights were turned down and most of us slept. We must have made a service stop but I can't recall it, but following that we were enroute to San Francisco.

The guys had been pestering the girl for most of the trip but eventually several of us went to sleep on the floor. The lights were down, and Dan David sat with the girl for most of the night talking. After he dozed off I noticed the girl was writing a letter or what I thought was a letter. When we were getting off the next morning she gave it to Dan and told him not to open it until we were at sea.

We were quartered in the St. Francis Hotel in San Francisco for four days. One of the kids got married while we were there. Their folks came out from the Midwest for that. We had nothing to do while waiting for our ship transport to show so Dan suggested we go out and walk around a bit taking in the sights. We did and sometime later came across a bookstore. Dan wanted to go in and found a book by Thorne Smith called *The Bishop's Jaegers* in which a bishop is shipwrecked on a nudist colony and is 'requested' to honor the "dress code". It was one of those times where every time Dan sat down to read we were disturbed and headed out someplace. He never got to read the book and the book went into the duffle bag as we marched aboard our naval transport.

We were finally taken over to Oakland and marched into a big liner that had once been a luxury liner. She belonged to the Dutch something like Akota Agona. We were on the boat deck because we were above the teaming thousands as they flooded onto the ship. They had men crammed in every imaginable place.

The cabin we were in had pipe racks made to sleep eight men. By some twist of fate I was the ranking man so I got the bottom bunk. I was the ranking man because I had a year in the draft before the war. David got the top bunk. Above his bunk was a big 12 inch iron pipe that ran the length of the ship.

We were the last men to come aboard so right after we were in place we heard whistles and people running around with much shouting in a flurry of action. We saw them take in all the mooring lines and there were no tugs in the area so the great ship got off the dock by herself. That crew made a difficult maneuver look easy but it didn't seem like much to me.

We passed under the bridge and made for the open sea. This ship had three great engines in it. One of the engines was broke but that didn't make any difference because we were going to run in convoy and convoy speed was slow. Night came and the ship was plowing ahead straight to the west. Dan had the late night shift and when we woke in the morning there were eleven transports in column. I never saw how or when we rendezvoused with them; we sailed out all alone and the next morning we are in a precise formation with every ship in station and destroyers darting in and out to keep the big ships in line.

Off to the sides and to front and rear were destroyers. They would slide by us at times and then disappear in the distance. It dawned on me the enemy would never be able to count on the warships to be in any particular place at any particular time thus making a submarine's shooting solution almost impossible. I knew destroyers had sensing devices that undoubtedly worked unceasingly to outsmart any enemy above, on, or below the surface.

The commander of the convoy was in a ship about a mile ahead and we were told he was a Commodore. The first excitement to occur happened when the Army Artillery unit was doing dry firing drills. This was on a big 5 inch rifle that was mounted on the fore deck. The navy was arming their merchant marine fleet and those ships drafted to serve. I am sure the rookie crew was a scratch crew made up of men that had other jobs as their main job but would serve as gun crew when needed, something we called additional duty.

I was sitting with my back to the port rail just idly watching them. They did a detail striping of the gun and cleaned, polished, oiled and reassembled the piece. The officer had them traverse and train the gun on ships in the convoy and any passing flotsam in the water. Then they ran through loading and dummy firing procedures and exercises. Finally they somehow got a live round in the gun and someone triggered it. I must have come 5 feet off the deck.

A 5"/38cal rifle is a big gun. It can fire a 55 pound shell to 37,000 feet straight up or 18,000 yards in surface fire. This gun was originally designed in 1933, was accepted by the navy in 1934 and was the standard small cannon on a whole fleet of ships until 1990. It was a very good weapon system and when it went off next to me it was a very loud weapons system. It took me several days to recover from that shock.

That shell traveled right alongside the column and landed just a few yards off the port side of the flagship where it went off. Black smoke started to erupt from the destroyers as they poured on the power and swung in curves towards the main body. In all the convoy, men were scrambling to get into clothes and race to battle stations. Bells and horns were ripping the air and red lights were flashing all over the ships. "Battle Stations" was being screamed over the loudspeakers and all through the ships, crews were frantically getting covers off guns and ammo was being rushed to position. On the transport, the best place for us during this drill was to do anything to stay out of the way as the sailors rushed by.

I knew that the accidental firing was no small matter and some Second Lieutenant was about to be roasted to a cinder. Careless errors are not tolerated in war.

Dan David was laying in his bunk much of the time since we left the port. He had the book with him. I was beginning to think that book was going to kill him.

It was full of humor and each time something funny came along David would convulse with laughter and his knees would snap up and his head and upper body would come up at the same time. His head would strike the big pipe and a great BONG would sound throughout the ship. I tried to get him to put the book away but he wouldn't do it. His forehead actually had a black and blue bruise on it he hit it so often. Of course to him – the harder he hit is head the funnier it was and there would soon be another BONG followed shortly by yet another.

This continued through a large part of the evening when he finally gave up reading exhausted and fell to sleep. The following night he started reading the book again and would just lose it - his head hitting the pipe again sending the great BONG throughout the ship. He continued reading and breaking up until a Chief with a repair crew in hand came barging into our suite. Seems he and his crew had been searching for the mechanical malfunction for two days.

The Captain of the ship was not quite as polite as the Chief was when he took Lieutenant David's book from him. As a guest in front of the Captain's desk, young Lieutenant David got to experience the full measure of a senior officer tearing a new one as they say. The Captain raved about submarines being in the area and how a regular BONG was advertising the ship's position and just begging for a torpedo. He reminded Dan that Keel Hauling was a Naval Tradition and he was a traditional man. He asked the XO if flogging was still on the books and the XO said he'd have to look it up. After a lengthily chewing out, the Captain took possession of the book and told Dan he could have it back when they reached Pearl Harbor. Dan reported back to the suite all mope eyed and sad faced saying the ship's captain wanted to read the book first. He was also moved to the bunk below his current position.

I have always wondered in later years how Dan could be the straight man in the comedy team Rowen and Martin. He broke up at nearly everything and by the time he was done laughing the entire group was laughing with him. And he always got into strange situations that upon reflection would break him up and were a riot as well. I never could understand how a man like that could be the straight man in a comedy show. But he was a master.

He also had the letter the hostess gave him as we were leaving the airplane. About the fourth day out he must have thought of it and had everybody notify our group to meet on deck to hear what she had written. We were all sitting around him when he started to read it aloud. Although I had only been with her a couple of hours I have thought of her many times. I would have given much if I could present her words here but I neither think nor speak in the beautiful way that she did.

Her first sentence has stuck in my memory all these years. "I pray that God will keep you safe." She had seen us scattered all over the floor sleeping and I'm sure the thought that we wouldn't always be able to rest like that when we wanted to the most was what drove her words. Her thoughts were brief but very powerful. In the couple of years that I was in close association with Dan this was the only time that I ever saw him choked up. There were others in that group who reacted the same way.

The ship was jammed with men; thousands upon thousands of them and it seemed that every one of them was in some kind of gambling game. The games went on day and night without stopping and you couldn't walk down a hallway without stepping on a few. A few men seemed to end up with all the money until only a couple of games were still going. One young man took all his winnings to the troop commander and asked him to put the money in the safe and not to let him have any of it back until he was leaving the ship. I heard that he eventually went broke and tried to get some of his horde from the commander but the CO wouldn't let him have it. The kid had a barrack bag full when he marched off the ship and an escort by the CO as he headed off to the Western Union to ship the money home. Everybody was paid in full before getting on the ship, most were broke upon leaving it.

The last 'event' on our voyage to Hawaii got me additional duty and a promotion to Flight Lieutenant (sort of). Two pigeons landed on the ship. They were completely exhausted and we were able to pick them up so I knew they were used to humans handling them. An older gent down the road from me had raised homing pigeons when I was a kid and I got to help him when I was small, thus I was some kind of expert in the maintenance of birds. Each bird was carrying a tiny capsule fastened to its leg. We decided to call the Troop Commander and see what should be done; he radioed for instructions after clearing communications with the ship's Captain.

Word came back for us to care for the birds but not to touch the capsules. The Major was standing looking at the birds. He asked if anybody knew what the birds ate. I, of course, opened my mouth and he said "Lieutenant you know what to do so you are the commander of this flight."

A couple of sailors built a cage for them and I watered and fed them. At Honolulu some people came aboard and two Lieutenants examined the capsules to see if they had been tampered. A soldier with a cage took the birds and with that I was relieved of my fowl duties.

One of the better memories of Draftee life in the Army was hot chow delivered to the field. Not only was the effort appreciated, the food was superb, well at least as I recall.

It was really amazing as to how much of our training was self-study (the M3 37mm cannon training) and here at Fort Knox with the .50. I am holding the safe end of the gun and at this time in my military career I would caution anyone being down range from the other end.

This is a photo from Luke Field where we did advanced fighter training. The caption is "Here's Hoping Fellas" and yes we were hoping.

And there was plenty of flying as well as class work and school room study and homework and you name it. At Chico we also got to perform physical training in 100 degree + weather.

And finally we got to move up to the Advanced Trainer the AT6 at Luke Air Base in Arizona, where we got to practice long distance navigation and flights, air gunnery, air bombardment, flight discipline and of course all the classroom work and study we could take. Night flying was commonly on the schedule.

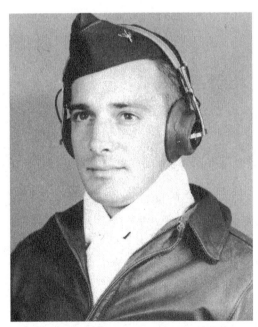

And then I graduated and they took my picture to send home to the newspaper in case they ever had to refer to something I might do in the war, me and 40,000 other fledging pilots. And yes I was the oldest cadet at the time.

HAWAII

19 February - 9 March 1943

The pilots were taken off first and loaded on trucks, which took us to Kaneohe, Naval Air Station. About 8 of us got off the trucks and officially joined the 73d PS. (Pursuit Squadron). The others went to other squadrons on the islands.

Dan was sent to a squadron across the island from me called Haleiwa. The Japs flew right over there when they attacked Pearl Harbor. That is where George Welch launched from and is credited with shooting down four aircraft on Pearl Harbor Day. His wingman Second Lieutenant Ken Taylor got two. Students of the war have told us all our forces only totaled twenty six kills and the majority were due to flak. I spoke to a man who knew, first hand, that a pilot from someplace else on the island got one in a P-36.

Our aircraft were older P-40Es. The closer we got to the shooting war the more decrepit the aircraft got. This time was a seasoning period for us. We practiced gunnery, dive bombing, and patrolling. We were put into groups with some of the older heads that had been around for a while. Most had been in combat and were rotated back for a break and they shared their bits and pieces of knowledge with us highlighting what brought them home alive. We worked with them for quite some time and it got to the point we actually questioned why the big rush to get us out here.

Many times we were sent out to sea to greet ships coming in from the states. The Navy figured Jap subs might stake out the harbor because of the heavy traffic there and we would fly cover for the ships when they got close. We were always looking for subs and it was good practice for our navigation skills.

One of those greetings was simply spectacular. Every service and every aircraft that could fly went on that mission. General SLA Marshal was coming to Hawaii and no expense or effort was spared to welcome him. It was a tremendous spectacle, and upon reflection a logistical and tactical miracle to coordinate that much aircraft and ground support from two services for that show. I hope he appreciated the effort but I never asked him.

One of our exercises was to dive bomb or skip bomb a rock off the shore. The P-40 was just about obsolete when the war started. In some respects it was poorly designed. It was very difficult to maintain the trim in flight and in a dive where speeds changed radically it had a serious effect on any gunnery you might be doing. Most pilots used heavy pressure on the left rudder to overcome the torque. It was a common saying "you can tell a P-40 pilot because his left thigh is so much larger than his right from holding the left rudder in."

One incident that resulted from that characteristic happened to a kid from Bellows field. That outfit had just been reequipped with brand new P-40-K aircraft. The man was making a dive-bombing run on the rock and his speed evidently got way up. He wasn't monitoring his attitude instrument and the ball was way off. When he sucked the stick back it must have been real hard. The bird snap rolled and the force was so great it bent 7 feet of one wing straight up in the air. He got the bird back on the ground but I'll bet he never forgot the needle and ball again.

The 73rd had been to Midway Islands, a fact that seems little known. The fighters must have been loaded on a carrier and then flown off when they got close to the field probably about 150 miles out. The Navy wouldn't want to show the carrier unnecessarily. The old heads in the squadron would tell anecdotes of their short stay out there.

We had a real tragedy about the middle of our training. One of the old pilots in the squadron was leading a four ship training mission doing formation flying. For reasons never to be known he led them into a cloud and flew right into the Pali Mountains killing them all.

One of the old heads took my flight out for an exercise against the US Navy and their coastal defense guys. The briefing had all the details and included the safety instructions including how to aim a pretend bomb at a target. We were going after a pillbox on the edge of a sugarcane field.

If the attack was real I would be carrying a 500 pound bomb and would be firing six 50 caliber machine guns. However it was a simulation and I would only fly through the planned exercise with no bomb or machineguns.

It was an unannounced attack on the Navy men in the pillbox. I came in from 12,000 feet and was indicating something close to 300 miles per hour. I made up my mind I was going to put my pretend bomb into a gun port and to do that I would have to get very close.

A gunner must never look at the sight reticle; you must always keep your focus on the target and super impose the reticle on the target. This is mandatory and is the difference between living and dying. When firing from a long way out it is not critical, but from close in, as I was doing, there isn't any room for error. At the speeds we were dealing with, fractions of seconds are all you have to rectify a mistake. The tinny voice of the old head came across the headphones with a "Ok Lieutenant, commence your run."

The altitude and attitude of the P-40 was proper, I checked the gages, the dive indicator, and made my quick shoulder check to ensure the dive path was clear both in front of the whirling prop and my 6 o'clock. I was ready, the plane was ready, it was time.

I pushed the nose over into a 40% dive, increased the throttle, and focused on the pillbox I was to simulate strafing. The P40's Allison engine's pitch changed from the heavy rumble of an unmuffled Harley Davidson to the classic high pitched Hollywood whine as the craft picked up speed and lunged towards the target.

I concentrated on the gun sight lining up the pit with the inner circle of the sight. Something in the back of my mind was keying me that I was doing something not quite right but for the life of me I could not figure out what the problem could be. My sixth sense was screaming so I did a quick check of the gages and dials on the control panel. The altimeter looked like a stop watch running backwards but that was to be expected, I was after all in a power dive throwing a 9,200 pound aircraft at full power at the ground.

That little voice was screaming in the back of my mind, but there was nothing wrong with the aircraft, so I overrode the warning and concentrated on the inner circle of the gun sight.

The sailors manning the gun pit started to bail out of the trench and beat feet from the area, and then it dawned on me. They were beating feet from an impact area. That little voice was not mine, it was a recalled instruction from one of the old heads – NEVER watch the gun sight, always concentrate on the target. I was too low, I was going to auger in to the gun pit at over 400 miles per hour without so much as even saying harsh words at the Japs let alone win the war. At that speed they wouldn't even look for the tiny pieces of my remains to ship home.

I saw flashes of the blue work uniforms as the sailors bailed out of the bunker and sucked the stick back hard very hard. My knuckles were white from the death grip I had on the yoke and every muscle in my back, legs and arms were straining to the max. I got over the pillbox but if that box had a coat of paint, I would have hit it. I laugh at those that don't believe in Guardian Angles, I had a whole battalion of them and I worked them overtime.

The ship sank below the box on the other side and hit in the sugar cane with a terrifying smash. A couple of feet lower and that big Allison engine would have gone like a bullet and taken out a block of wooden shacks at the other side of the field, but I managed to regain control and fly level 8 feet above the ground.

There were other factors involved here that contributed to keeping me alive. First: fighter aircraft were built to withstand eleven positive G's. I am convinced that anything less and the plane would have disintegrated especially when it struck the cane. Second: the airline hostess' prayer to keep us safe had to be the only possible answer as to why I was still breathing. Saving me from my stupidity was too much for mere mortals and I had to have help from outside of this world.

I somehow managed to get a bit more lift and started climbing for altitude. Despite the impact on the cane I rejoined the old head and slotted back into formation. I glanced over in his direction and although he was a 100 yards away I could feel his glare of pure unadulterated hatred. One did not need pilot's vision to see that I was not on his favored guy list at all and if he could get his pistol out he would have shot me.

We went back to the strip and I made a normal landing. When I was getting out of the ship I had a couple of steps and a handhold to use. I was still holding the handhold when my foot touched the ground. I was hit by a titanic shock and I thought my arm had been ripped off. Later I found that when the bird hit the sugar cane it tore the static discharge wire off. That caused the store of electricity to discharge through my body because the wire was gone. It was a very large charge and I thought my arm was torn off. Anyone that saw the incident gave me no sympathy, especially the ground crews because that P40 was obviously paying me back for the harsh way I had treated the machine.

If I expected any sympathy from the old head that lead the flight I was off in never never land dreaming impossible fantasies. The pain in my arm and shoulder were just the beginning. I needless to say heard quite a bit about my attack on the box back at the strip. I pretty much did a lot of listening and not a whole lot of talking. Listening is always much better when the one doing the listening is at the position of attention and the speaker is 2 inches away from his face screaming in such a loud voice it probably woke the emperor up all those miles away in Japan.

I did wonder when the man was going to stop yelling long enough to breathe but apparently that is not a necessity when ripping a stupid boot loot flyboy hotshot junior birdman who's too big for his britches. And those are the polite words I can use in this publication. Polite words were a very small segment of his speech. I did learn about the cost of the P40 Warhawk several times, evidently the plane is much more valuable to the war effort than hotshot flyboys etc.

Needless to say I did learn a valuable lesson that day and in later postings actually became a fairly good shot, using the sight reticle to get on target and then immediately getting out of the site and watch the bullet strike on the target. As odd as it may seem I actually became the squadron gunnery officer for the new pilots.

I never saw the old head again, he shipped back to the States that evening and I got my orders to move to the South Pacific.

WE GO SOUTH

9 - 20 April 1943

The day came to ship off to the combat zones and we were loaded into a B-24 for the flight to the south. We knew this time we were going to war and I definitely had some butterflies flying around in my stomach. There is nothing worse than knowing you are headed into the breach as Shakespeare would say and just having to sit around waiting to do it.

At least we were going to war in a war bird. The Consolidated B-24 Liberator was the less pretty main bomber in the US strategic air bombardment war but actually had significant advantage over the B-17 which was used in all the movies. I do admit the Flying Fortress was a sharper looking machine than both the B-24 and the later B-29 bombers.

The US made roughly 7,000 more Liberators than Flying Forts and the B-24 had a larger bomb load, roughly 2000 pounds, longer range nearly 1400 miles, and better defensive armament than the B-17. Speed and ceiling go to the B-17, but the differences are miniscule. My next door neighbor flew 24s and swore by them and never could figure why those ships were not the subject of some Hollywood major release. I told them they were not sexy and thought he was going to hit me. Bomber pilots have no sense humor.

The crew was civilian; this again was a war expedient in that trained bomber pilots were running bomber missions, not flying spare parts and rookie bird men around the Pacific. It also meant we were headed to a rear area as those civilians were too expensive to get shot up over the front lines. Either way our transport pilots appeared to be a bit green and they couldn't have had much time in any aircraft let alone a B-24.

We took off and everything went fine until we got to Fiji. We landed and had to unload our personal gear so the ground crews could unload some of the supply on the plane. When I handed my kit down to a Marine on the ground he nonchalantly tossed it into a pile at the side of the strip. I had a bottle of Old Crow in the bag and it broke. The Marines homed on the smell and took my underwear and socks out and squeezed the whisky out into their mouths. They then thanked me for the drink.

The whisky was supposed to be trading material for souvenirs. I had been briefed to leave anything else but to bring all the whisky I could squeeze in my bag because that would go over well with those folks that actually had something worth trading.

The next morning I walked out to the aircraft and got a real fright. During the night the ground crews evidently added some more cargo to that with which we had arrived. When we got aboard at Hickam Field we had to sit on top of four engine crates. There were lots of lesser boxes in the big bird also.

A B-24 has a standard three wheel landing gear, two huge main wheels and a nose wheel. With a normal load the rear of the plane would always be clear of the ground and in a parallel alignment. Well this one wasn't and I knew enough to know that wasn't right. The rear gunner position was nearly touching the ground and the nose gun position was at a 45 degree angle to the ground. That plane just didn't look right let alone look like it could fly. Several of us tried to get them to take one of the engines out but we wasted breath.

The ground crew said they couldn't with the comment that the guy who approved the load knew what he was doing. I noted that they were not going to ride in the plane and that didn't get any response whatsoever. The ground crew brought a pump out and added more pressure to the tires to get a slight bit of level to the plane. That was stupid because those tires were all ready as hard as rock with their normal pressure.

The air crew had the final say in whether or not to take off but they were afraid to say anything, I did mention they were green about the gills. When it became apparent that no one was going to listen to us we boarded the plane and sat as close to the cockpit wall as possible. If we would have had a rear gunner we would have tipped the plane right back into the tail dragging attitude.

The airstrip had a drop off at the end which was around two hundred feet. When they got us all loaded the pilot started up and did the only thing he could think of. He taxied as far out into the overrun as he could. Just like the overloaded DC2 guy had done in the previous episode. He lined up and set his brakes. He sat there with all four of the Pratt and Whitney Wasp engines running at full throttle. If there was any possible way to squeeze any more horse power out of them he was doing it. I'm sure he was talking it over with his copilot but decided to go. He had burned off about twenty gallons of gas roughly 150 pounds and those monster engines had to be at the point of overheating. He released the brakes and the Liberator began to roll.

Speed builds up slowly in the big ships. We ground along and were getting close to the end of the runway but we were now going fast enough that there was no way to stop. We knew he couldn't abort now. When he tried to rotate, the tail immediately hit the ground and he couldn't use his engines' power to help lift his aircraft.

The guy hit the over run and just kept going at full power. I give him credit for his next move, we fell off the cliff and he kept it straight and level. We must have lost 70 to 100 feet of altitude but he picked up enough speed before hitting the water. He flew right on the water for about three miles before starting a very gentle climb. He got to altitude and set the cruise. He looked back to ensure his passengers and cargo were ok and looked as though he could have really used a sip of my socks.

Our trip ended at Noumea, New Caledonia where the B-24 made a normal landing with no weight issues as the fuel was fairly well used up.

We didn't stay at Noumea very long before being shipped to a strip out in the country called 30 Mile where we were checked out in P-39s. I am quite sure the one I flew was an early model. It must have been in very good shape because it handled so well. It was light on the controls and after horsing the P-40 around the 39 was a pleasure.

The P-39 Airacobra is a perfect example of a well-designed highly functional, superb war machine which was "improved" until it was basically nonfunctional. In 1938 when the plane was introduced to the Air Corps it had a turbo boosted Allison V12 water cooled engine that moved that bird at 390mph at medium altitude. At 390mph it was the fastest fighter of its time in the world.

It had several astounding design innovations which when combined made the aircraft a joy to fly. The engine was mounted behind the pilot in what is called a mid-fuselage configuration. This novel idea puts the weight of the engine in the aerodynamic center of the plane and allows for greater maneuverability and allows for heavier nose armament. Additionally, the cockpit was a dream – well laid out, comfortable, great vision, and plenty of space. It had car doors and a fixed canopy which was strange upon first glance but was actually quite easy to get used to.

The most reliable part of the plane that had the fewest failures (I have not heard of one) was the drive shaft that ran the prop. The engine applied power to a reduction gear that spun up the propeller; the spin shaft ran directly between the pilot's legs.

There was one other unusual configuration at the time and that was the tricycle landing gear. Most fighters used the "tail dragger" configuration and that was what we all learned to fly on – Ryan, Steerman, BT13, and AT6 were all tail draggers. Most of the bombers were moving over to a tricycle configuration – but I already mentioned their pilot's lack of humor.

Any way the fighter demoed to the Air Corps inspectors was one hot machine. The one we eventually took to combat was "improved" to the point of near uselessness. First improvement was to pull the blower off the engine (the turbocharger) which had the effect of losing power and the ability to fly at high altitudes. Congress didn't want to expand the Army Air Corps budget just as the country was coming out of the Great Depression. The rationale was the Army Air Corps could not have two brand new high altitude fighters, so the turbo was pulled from the P-39 Airacobra but left in the P-38 Lightening.

As soon as the whiz kids pulled the supercharge turbos off the engine, they added more drag to the plane by moving the radiators from the fuselage to the wings and they added 2200 pounds of weight to the plane by putting in self-sealing tanks, armor plate, bullet proof glass, .30 caliber machineguns and a 37mm cannon. Granted all good stuff for a fighter plane but it still needs to have power. The effects of these modifications were the plane could still fly and was a stable gun platform but lost significant climbing and maneuvering speed and ability.

So since it needed more power and couldn't have a turbo because some admin weenie said the USA couldn't have two supercharged turbo fighters, the only solution was to dump in a bigger engine with yet again more weight. This disaster was accomplished without modification to the air frame which severely limited the plane's ceiling and maneuvering ability. About the only thing the plane could do real well was dive. It was often said that the final "improved" versions of the P-39 had "the flying characteristics of a rock, a poorly thrown rock."

The final version where they fixed everything was designated the P-69 King Cobra and we gave all of those to the Russians.

So we went to fight the Empire of Japan in fighter aircraft that didn't have much of a chance against the more maneuverable Japanese fighters. If we were higher than the Japs (very rare) we could dive on them and get a gun pass, pretty much just like a drive by shooting. If we got them yea for us, if not it was keep diving because none of the lighter Japanese aircraft could stay with the 39 in a full power dive.

Unfortunately we had to learn that one the hard way. General Chennault of the First American Volunteer Group – otherwise known as the Flying Tigers, had discovered it was suicide to turn with a Zero fighter in a P40, which was much more maneuverable than the 39. Trying to do that in a 39 was simply stupid, but it is the natural instinct and the chivalrous thing to do. We learned real quick there was nothing chivalrous about air combat. The more the P39 was used the worse its reputation became.

I quickly found out why the little plane was in such disrepute. Range was very short – 650 miles without drop tanks and it couldn't do much at altitude. It had a reputation for tumbling but I couldn't make it do that and never saw one so I can't confirm it. Some folks complained you couldn't use the cannon in a dive and lastly the 39 was accused of losing its tail. I never saw that either but knew of it happening several times. None of those pilots survived.

The allegations made by several writers that the 39 was slow are a puzzle to me. The P-39D with the 1170hp engine and the Curtis three blade electric prop was the fastest airplane in the Air Corps inventory. I have personally proved that on several occasions. That didn't hold true at high altitude because the other first line aircraft had super-chargers and we didn't.

The plane was a low wing plane. That being the case, if the horizontal stabilizer came off, no matter how, the aircraft would go nose down so hard that the pilot would be crushed against the canopy and his neck would surely be broken. The nose over would then be so exaggerated that the wings would fold under the plane.

Many men loosened the harness for comfort. I always flew with my harness as tight as I could make it. One could get out of the plane if it got in trouble, the "car" doors had an emergency release that allowed the wind stream to blow the doors off the cockpit and it was roomy enough to move around and get out, but you could not get out if you were unconscious and no one could get out if the wings collapsed.

I guess the biggest complaint against the P39 was summed up by one of Japan's leading aces to survive the war. Saburo Sakai wrote that whenever a flight of P-39s was encountered it was a good opportunity for the inexperienced pilots to get some firing practice. He said the P39 was an easy kill. That is not the kind of aircraft one wants to take into battle.

There is however one small fact that blows away all theories of P39 unworthiness and Japanese superiority and that fact is that by December 1942, Fifth Air Force claimed 80 Japanese aircraft of all types for roughly the same number of P39s lost. A one to one against the Zero – the 39 was at a disadvantage, one to one against a Betty or a Kate, and the Japanese were at a disadvantage. But the complaints continued so the mission was somewhat changed for the 39 and it was mostly used as a ground attack weapon.

It is appropriate to explain the administration of the Air Forces at least as it happen during my time in the services as it can be confusing. When I applied for pilot school upon graduation of high school I applied to the Commanding General United States Army Air Corps. In the 1920 it became somewhat apparent that those new machines needed special coordination and logistics support. It wasn't going to work to have each Army Division have its own little aircraft section so the US Army built a specialized corps of planes and equipment and men to service, fly, and administer them.

Thus came the birth of the USAAC on July 2, 1926. To the Air Corps' credit, almost all of the tactics, equipment, function, training, supply, maintenance process and procurement procedures had been worked out by the Air Corps before the administrative dragon of a rapidly expanding "unique" service overwhelmed a Corps level staff.

Thus was born the United States Army Air Forces as a sub-branch of the US Army. This reorganization was in June 1940 but the Army Air Corps was not fully disbanded until March 1942. So some confusion was built into the transition period and the start of the war did nothing to enhance the process. Bottom line is that by the time I was commissioned in January 1943, all Army Air Corps groupings and labels had been converted to USAAF which would last until September 17, 1947 when the independent service, the USAF, was born.

With the re-designation of the AAC to the USAAF, pursuit squadrons were to be replaced with the new designation of fighter squadrons, however there were tons of supplies and letter head that still used the term Pursuit rather than Fighter and throughout most the war Pursuit Squadron and Fighter Squadron could pretty much be used interchangeably. The aviation industry was slower to adapt in that all our air craft continued to be labeled as P (P-39, P-40, P-51...). Later in my career with the USAF when jet aircraft were introduced the F designation became effected, (F-86, F101, F4, F15...).

GUADALCANAL

10 April - 29 May 1943

P-39s were faster than the P-40 and they were a pleasure to fly. They were lighter on the controls and had much less torque than the P-40, and the P-39 had the heaviest wing loading of any craft in service. When we finished checking out at 30 Mile we were loaded in a transport and flown to Espiritu Santo. We were taken out in the jungle to a cleared place where over a hundred P-39s were stored.

We were told to pick any one we wanted and it would be ours forever more. It was like being a kid in the candy store. I saw one in the bunch that looked like new so I went and checked it out. Several of the pilots had worked on airplanes as enlisted men and they didn't spend time looking at the planes but instead studied the maintenance forms. They got the best planes on the lot but they didn't look as good as mine.

Later we fired up and taxied out for takeoff. I learned later once you strapped that bird to your behind you were mated forever. We met a B-25 enroute to our new base and I thought we were providing an escort for the bomber. As it turned out, the bomber was our guide to our duty station as the brass really didn't want to lose 8 new pilots and more importantly 8 rebuilt P39s before they had even checked in at their new duty station. We had a non-event flight, perfect weather, smooth flying conditions and stunningly beautiful scenery. The ocean was a pale light blue, the islands' beaches were the purest white and the jungles were deep green often with rivers flowing and lakes opening the canopy. Streams and lakes were the deepest blue and perfectly clear. It truly was a Pacific Paradise – well except for the war.

We landed at Guadalcanal and that place had been hard used. Wrecks littered the sides of the strip and were saved for spare parts, broken half sunk ships were on the beaches where the Japanese had tried to counter attack the Marine landing in August 1942, and supplies and maintenance sheds and boxes were stacked all over the area. And despite the best efforts of the camp commandant, other than the flight line, there was garbage all over the place.

I met the engineering officer when I got to Guadalcanal and the first thing he asked me was where were the forms for my bird? I reached in and handed him a stack of papers in a record book and my clipboard. He went over the records with me and here is what I learned. The airplane had been shot down twice in the Fiji Islands and someone had also messed it up pretty good after it came out of its first depot rebuild (there were two rebuilds).

We identified my ship as a P-39D2-63 as now configured which meant some of my parts would have to be special ordered. Only 160 P-39D-2s were built before the next sub-variant was ordered. This aircraft had the most powerful engine ever installed in P-39s. It was almost two hundred horse power stronger than any other ship in the squadron. No one could guess how that engine got to our depot, but it had and someone had jury rigged my ship to handle the larger engine – an Allison V-1710-63 which produced 1,325 horse power.

I guess I don't have to mention that I was somewhat horrified at my choice of fighter. I should have realized that the reason it was so shiny was because it was fresh off the rebuild line and something bad had happened to put it on the rebuild line in the depot. After my brief with the maintenance officer I joined my fellow pilots and headed off to get checked in at the various squadron and group offices; Operations, Personnel, and Logistics, the S shops, and then found my billet space. I threw my duffle bag in an empty cot and headed over to headquarters to meet the squadron CO. He was off on a mission and there were no officers in the headquarters.

When I checked into the supply office I was given a patch of a rooster with boxing gloves on the end of his arms (he had no wings) and was told to sew this patch on the left center of my flight jacket. The rooster was the official logo of the squadron and we were called the "Fighting Cocks." That logo was personally drawn by Walt Disney, the group that came over before us were eating dinner in a big fancy restaurant in LA, kind of their last great meal for a while kind of dinner. They spied Walt and wander over to talk to him. One of the guys asked Walt if he had any ideas for a squadron logo and Walt pulled out a pen and drew the logo on one of the napkins. The pilots loved it and one of the guys took it down to a print shop the next morning and got a hundred made up. Everyone thanked Walt and one of the guys heard Walt tell the waiter that he'd used a napkin and needed to have that added to his bill. He would have paid for the pilots dinner but they had already paid.

I had some time to spare and I hiked around looking at what sights interested me. From our Ops Quonset hut I could see the beach and there were two ships beached there. I walked down to look at the rusted and mangled ragged wrecks. The year before they probably were pristine commercial vessels drafted into the Japanese navy and shiny and clean, that's when it dawned on me just how damaging the jungle was to manmade constructions, iron rusted, wood rotted, and concrete crumbled.

The US Army calls those kinds of ships expendable. They were apparently designated as throw away ships to be grounded on the shore to let the troops get off in the attack. I saw some holes in both of them and there was not much worthy of exploration. I looked at the water and it was so clear that it almost seemed not to be there. I put my hand in the water and it was toasty warm. I stripped down to my shorts and went in. I wandered around the sand bottom and kept feeling hard objects under foot. Finally I ducked down and pulled one out. It was an unexploded mortar shell. I almost fainted. Here I was wading around in all that stuff and some of it was probably waiting to go off if disturbed. Using the utmost care I got out.

The Lunga River was only a short distance up the beach. Our guys would fly all day and then get their rifles and dig in along the river with the Infantry at night. The Japs were over there and there was plenty of shooting across that river even in April of 1943, despite the declaration that the island was secure in February of 1943.

One of the guys in my class, Dudley Clark of Salem Massachusetts, survived all the witch jokes in flight training and after indoctrination had been sent to North Africa flying P40s. He was shot down by a pair of German Messerschmitt Bf109s and in the crash his legs were horribly mutilated, eventually having to be amputated. He was shipped to a hospital in Boston where he wrote regularly to one of our guys.

In one of the letters was a big newspaper clipping. It was a big picture of our squadron pilots all grouped around and on a P-39. We had our rifles as the photo was taken right before we were heading off to the river. The caption said 'Marine Pilots in Guadalcanal'. All Dud Clark wrote on it was 'when did you guys transfer?'

When our group of new pilots rolled in, a like number of the old heads were rotated back to the states. That was a fairly common thing for the early groups as they had definitely done their job. Later in the war when they transitioned all the P-39 squadrons to the P-38 Lightening, that rotation back to the States thing was a fond memory. We were involuntarily extended twice and made the mistake of voluntarily extending once. Many of the men who went stateside when we arrived were killed doing crazy things.

Two of them were assigned to Republic Aviation as check pilots. As we heard it aircraft coming out of the factory had to be flight checked by the Army, before the Army accepted them. Two of our ex pilots were mesmerized by the idea that they could be the first men to go through the sonic barrier. Many people in those days believed it was only a matter of having enough power to do it. Well these men thought the big P-47 Thunderbolt was the ship that could and they both tried and were killed. There are some specific construction and design requirements that are needed in a plane capable of breaking the sound barrier, the P47 didn't have them.

I did finally get checked in and got to meet the CO later that night. It was a cursory event in that he was busy moving out of the CO slot but he did look me over and assigned me a flight operation the next morning. I would join two old heads in a patrol over the Solomon Sea and the Coast of Malaita Island in a real live Dawn Patrol, just like the movie with Errol Flynn.

The patrol was not a big deal to the old heads but it was my first combat patrol so I paid a bit more attention to the briefing in the Operations hut. I would be the third man, the tail end Charlie so to speak because the normal flight for that patrol was two ships. Our intelligence didn't have any specific concerns for the area but it was one of those patrols you go on to make sure the enemy had no surprises for us.

It dawned on me for the first time that tomorrow morning I would mount my aircraft and go into hazard's way. For the first time I could meet people that wore a different colored uniform who would take whatever weapons were available –air, ground, and sea, and try to cause me harm. Their sole purpose in life was to shoot me down in flames and if they did that to enough American pilots they could win this thing. No, I did not sleep well that night.

The schedule was routine for the old heads and would become routine for me but for the first mission it was all new. We had wakeup call at 330AM and dressed and shaved before heading over to the chow hall. Breakfast was at 4AM and briefing was at 4:30 and walk around aircraft inspection followed immediately after the brief. 5AM saw the engines turning over, com checks and final details before takeoff, by 515 we were wheels up winging our way to the patrol area. It was real important to get at the patrol area as the sun was coming up, we wanted to be east of the area patrolling west so that if any enemy craft were spotted we would have the sun behind our backs.

Chow was powered eggs, some SPAM and a bowl of oatmeal, hot coffee of course. The briefing was where we were assigned patrol areas, expected contact, enemy disposition, radio frequency and call signs to use, and if any friendlies were going to be in the area. I had taken copious notes until I saw the old heads and basically all they wrote down was the radio freq. Most wrote them on the palm of their hand.

The walk to the flight line was roughly 700 to 1000 yards. In that time the old heads tried to dump 7 months of fighting knowledge into my head. The one thing they highly stressed over and over was that if we found a Jap plane we'd jump it by making a power dive and hosing the thing with every weapon on the ship, 30 cal, 50 cal, and 37mm cannon. If it blew up or flamed – good for us, if not just keep power diving at full speed. When we were several miles away we could climb back to altitude and come back to see if we could get another strike. We would not repeat NOT dog fight them.

We got to Fighter 4, our strip on Henderson Field where the ground crews had been prepping our birds. My brand new shiny one was last in line and I immediately started my walk around. Eventually all this became completely routine but to get a modern fighter into the air, one needed a preoperational check list and a preflight checklist. It's not like the movies, there is more to start up than "Switch is on" "Contact". I found the smarter old heads that seemed to come back from mission after mission always used those checklists. I started using it on my first flight and never missed one since; even scrambles allow enough time for cursory checks.

When you first mount the P39, basically every switch except the battery and the night light need to be turned off. Ground crews are especially concerned that the wing and fuselage machineguns switches are off as well as the cannon switch. The preflight checklist has those items right at the top of the list. Next item is to set the generator to the on position and set the parking brakes. The plane is now ready for the start engine sequence.

With the engine ignition switch set to off the ground crew pulls the propeller blades making two or three full cycles. This gets the oil to the cylinders and the plane is now ready to start. The ground crew is waved off and now the pilot is on his own. Next steps are to turn on the battery switch and turn the ignition switch to the "Both" position. This allows one final check of the fuel state, the carburetor air, and the coolant gages.

Then we have to set the mixture control to the idle range and turn on the booster pump to prime the engine. The throttle is cracked about one inch, and the electric booster pump is then turned off.

The engine start uses an inertial fly wheel, to get that wound up you press the inertia pedal with the heel of your foot and hold it until it hits a high pitched whine. At that moment you engage the starter by tipping the starter pedal forward, which will spin the prop and fire the engine. You have to hold the starter in position until you get a regular firing sequence then clear the starter and push the mixture control to full rich.

The engine is now running at normal warm up speed. We let the engine turn over at 1400 rpms until the temperature gage came up to 80 degrees and the coolant rose to 180. This normally happened within 2 minutes of startup and could not be maintained for more than 5 minutes without damaging the engine.

A quick radio check with the tower and inter flight alternate radio frequency check; and the lead ship started taxing down the runoff to the strip. The second old head followed basically on the lead's tail and I followed a distant third. The two old heads flipped on their landing lights and roared off the strip together, one tucked inside the other. I waited for them to clear the strip and then followed a bit more cautiously.

We headed east and climbed to about 18000 feet which was about the top limit of our non-turbocharged engines. With a rate of climb at 3,333 feet per minute it would take us roughly 6 minutes to achieve that altitude. We never went much above 18,000 feet even though the plane was rated for 35,000 as the service ceiling. Without a turbo she just pretty much sat there. Old bombers and transports could outfly us at 18,000 which was downright embarrassing for a fighter pilot. When we escorted transports we used to have them fly at 12,000 feet where we could actually be protective.

We assumed a line abreast formation which is each plane lines up in a line with the other and then spread out approximately 5 miles from each other. We flew east to west and saw nothing. With a range of only 650 miles without drop tanks we could not loiter very long, roughly 2.5 hours which in that plane was just about the limit of creature comfort.

We tooled around the ocean and took a couple of sightings over Malaita and then headed back. We made a normal touch down and taxied off the strip to our staging areas. I took out my board and wrote down all the maintenance specifics of the flight and then headed off to the operations shop to give my after action report. That was my first combat flight. I never flew with that team again, both men rotated off the island within the week.

Thus started our operations off the Canal, unfortunately for us most of the other operations were not so pacific. Most of what we did was to fly recon missions and patrols until we had a bit of time under our belt. I was mildly relieved as Guadalcanal was still a hot spot, folks were attacking from and to the island and combat was a daily occurrence but it was not the slugfest I was expecting for the first couple of weeks. I met the Squadron CO but he was off on an important mission – that of transferring the squadron to the new CO Major Morris Hecht, so we didn't have much time together.

The battle for Guadalcanal officially was from the initial landing on August 7th 1942 to 9 February 1943. The Japanese army conceded the island and withdrew the majority of their remaining troops by 7 February 1943 and the US declared victory two days later. Unfortunately for us there were still plenty of Japs on the island and the Navy and Air Forces made routine bombing and shelling attacks on the island. We looked at the island is secured memo and wondered if anyone had given a copy to the Japs cause they still seemed to be interested in fighting over it.

We operated out of Henderson field and our area of responsibility was the Canal, Solomon Islands, Florida Islands and the Slot. Hecht saw that I was going to be a work in process so he assigned me to his best flight leader – Orval Collins. Collins and I became best buddies despite our rank differences, Collins was a Captain and I a mere Second Lieutenant, but I was older than him and we had similar backgrounds. He taught me a lot about flying.

We weren't there very long when I was called in to see Collins who was acting CO for Hecht and he told me I was first up for an R&R. I was surprised but happy; I later found I was taking a slot from the guy that I had replaced who had rotated back to the States. I don't think he was too upset about the trade.

I packed my stuff and caught the courier in the morning. The flight to Wards Drome near Port Moresby, New Guinea was uneventful. I checked in and was assigned a bed for the night. When I walked into the tent there was a young Captain sitting there writing a letter. He stood up and shook hands with me and introduced himself as Tom Lanpheir. I didn't know it at that moment but he was the man credited with shooting down Yamamoto. He had been relieved and on his way home.

I was instructed to report to the Load Master in the morning on the flight line for the continuation flight to Australia. I did that and he pointed to a Clip Wing B-26. "That's yours." he said.

I had heard that a complete Group of those aircraft had been lost in combat and due to mechanical failures. The only two left in New Guinea had been converted to passenger carriers. I told the Load Master I would wait for another ride.

He said: "You can't do that. You take your turn or you don't go."

I told the man, an Aussie limited duty officer, "Sir I won't ride in that." He shrugged his shoulders and said "Then you don't go."

He went down his list and called a name and a young Lieutenant stepped up. "Lieutenant you got a seat. Get aboard they are ready to go."

The kid thanked him and boarded. They buttoned up and the engines started to wind up. Those giant radial engines always seemed to me to be reluctant to go, almost like they are lazy. These were no different.

Soon both were running and just sounded like enormous power. I can't remember watching her roll out but turned when she started to roll for takeoff. Just as she broke ground, she pitched left only a few feet off the ground so the pilot had no chance to feather the prop. He might have been able to level off if he had just a couple of seconds but he didn't.

The wing hit the ground and the plane started a cartwheel until every drop of gas in that airplane ignited in a fraction of an instant. The explosion was horrific and the sound could be heard in the town 5 miles away. I saw some Aussie soldiers helping the Load Master off of the tarmac as he had fainted and I never saw him again. I was very sick as I watched the crash crews race to the scene but there was nothing to do for those men.

They put me in an old DC-2 the next morning. There seemed to be a lot of them around. This flight was slow and dreary but made me feel very comfortable.

I had seen the Aussie Commandos at Wards Drome when they were bringing them out of New Ireland and New Britain Islands. They were the roughest men I had ever seen. They had lived off the land much of the time and were without medical supply, food, and clothing. About the only thing on them that was not rotted thorough were their weapons which were in immaculate condition. I can imagine those men with Malaria, Dysentery, and every kind of fever and jungle rot, yet they continued the fight against the Japs.

Their hair was grown wild except where cut with a knife. I heard one spectator say "no one knows what they have done and no one will for they will never tell." What an amazing group of men they were.

On the DC-2 was one of those men. He was semi invalid. He was helped aboard and was placed in the rear of the passenger compartment. It was awkward. I don't think he was comfortable with a planeload of officers. I didn't feel comfortable with him tucked out of the way in the back. I wondered how he could have got in such an outfit because he seemed too old.

I had heard that they were all volunteers so that might explain it. It was obvious he was beset with the tropical diseases as well as several wounds: Lord knows how many and how bad. The old transport ground away until somebody said: "there she is." meaning the Australian coast.

Someone saw the old soldier was trying to get up and helped him. A couple of men got him to a window, which was close to me. I would bet a great deal that this man had never pleaded or begged to be relieved from any duty because he was hurt or sick or tired almost beyond bearing. Fighting with guns and grenades and knives and clubs or anything else at hand was his forte. He had never complained about his situation. But now with his head two feet from me tears rolled down his face. Just seeing the blue line of the coast of home broke him down. We made a seat for him so he could look out the window. We landed at Townsville and an ambulance came for him.

From Townsville we were ordered to a train. That was an old narrow gage track and of course it was a steam locomotive. We lumbered through the country stopping at farms and every little village and we got a steady dose of coal smoke. We could put up the window to block some of the smoke and bake ourselves due to the heat or we could open the windows, draw some drafts of air but got some of the engine smoke in the car. Brisbane was 1200 miles from Townsville and we decided it was better to smell of smoke and have an occasional breath of fresh air.

We had an overnight stay at Brisbane. We couldn't find a place to sleep so someone sent us to the Salvation Army and they sent us some place where we were assigned cots. The lady who signed us in gave each of us four empty tomato cans. We asked what they were for and she told us. 'Fill the cans half full of water and set the cot's legs in the middle of the water otherwise the ants would eat you.'

We paid forty cents for the bed. I remember the man I was with was named McCulla, he was another hick just like me. It was too early to go to bed so we walked around the town until we saw the movie theater. Mac said "this is a good one. Let's go in here. "

There were many commercial ads presented before the main attraction. One was a Coca Cola ad introduced by a gorgeous girl. I can't remember the title of the movie we went to see but I can recall that girl. Mac gave a "whoo- hoo" and I thought the same thing. We watched the movie, had a coke and headed back to the Salvation Army place for the night.

The next day we left for Sydney. Even on R&R they have to process you to ensure the right person is on vacation. Processing in was in a big office building of a huge department store titled David Jones. The owner had provided the space as part of his war effort.

At the counter we could see a very big room that looked like a different business. There were dozens of young women employed there and we thought it would be nice to have some company. The lady in charge assisted the clerks in processing and I drew her for my turn. When she finished she asked if I wanted to meet a young lady for a date. She said, "don't make any mistake. These are nice girls." Any friendships started up with the ladies were to be platonic and not romantic, and for the most part they were.

Mrs. James was her name and she was lovely. She said many of the girls were married and their husbands were in the Far East or Africa fighting. The girls needed recreation just as we did. She also told me the girls had given pictures to be put in an album and I could look at that if I would like to.

As we were talking I was looking at the amazing sight in the next office. One of the young women was close to us. Something about her seemed familiar to me and I said "Mrs. James How about that girl?"

"Oh yes, she is a lovely girl. Here is what we will do. I will bring her over and introduce you. You tell her you have a ticket to the tea dance Sunday afternoon. Ask her if she would she care to go."

Mrs. James brought the girl over and introduced us. The girl was very pretty and I'm sure she sensed that I was a very mixed up man. She said she would like to go to the dance on Sunday which gave me time to get my uniform cleaned and pressed. (Haircut and barber shave too)

When she got close to me I realized she was the girl who made the commercial in Brisbane. When I asked her if in fact she had made the commercial she confirmed that it was she and that it was a rather fun event. We hit it off immediately and I was the number one leader of her fan club, Mac being number 2. We got to a first name basis hers being Pat and mine being Lucky.

The tea dance was at two o'clock and was in a gigantic ballroom. It suddenly dawned on me I didn't know how to dance. I was going to have to tell her before we went in. The girl just laughed. "About half of you Americans don't know how to dance. We will have fun and I will teach you." She knew how to get me relaxed. I took her to dinner a couple of times and then to the Stars and Bars nightclub.

It was there I ran into George Welch. He had had much too much to drink and was getting a bit boisterous. I tried to ignore him as by now I was a very 'accomplished' dancer and I didn't want to leave.

Pat said we have to take him to his room. I said I didn't get him drunk but she insisted. "Other men who have had too much combat do the same thing and we have to look out for them." It was at that moment that my respect and admiration for her increased many times over.

At the dance I talked with another girl about Pat as we were dancing. She told me that Pat was the leading model in Australia. Her picture was everywhere. Everyone had to have a job associated with the war effort that's why she was working at David Jones. My ten days were up and we got on a transport for New Guinea. At Moresby we caught the courier back to the 'Canal. Just as I got back Collins headed out.

It was at that time Collins met a lovely girl in Australia who was not married to some soldier in Africa or Asia. The word got around and everybody treated her special. Any one on R&R got an additional duty to stop by her house and drop off some gifts and letters Collins had for her. Everyone that did was treated to a full home cooked meal by either the girl or her mother and an exceptional time and if needed a spare bedroom and laundry services. Her name Merele Faire was almost as pretty as she was. She was quite the catch and everyone told Collins how lucky he was.

Back at work it seemed to me it was only to keep us occupied. The US had moved unopposed into the Russell Islands about 60 miles north of the Canal and immediately started making another couple of air strips. We got up early every day and flew a patrol. After that we would strafe somewhere or drop some bombs or escort a few transports. That's when we had a slow day, some days had more action than needed or wanted and that usually was when we'd strafe and bomb airfields, harbors, or enemy shipping. The Japs liked those things and put lots of cannon and machineguns around them.

For me the worst was Tonolei harbor. Tonolei harbor is on the south eastern portion of Bougainville and looks like an elongated small case n lying on its side. The harbor is sheltered by heavily vegetated mountains on the sea to a height of 250 feet and the island side with mountains near 450 feet. Fauro and Shortland islands are located to the south east and south west respectively. The harbor is completely covered in heavy jungle and there are several rivers that flow into the bay. It is backed by high densely wooded hills particularly on the Eastern flank, and the Japanese defended the harbor with both ground mounted antiaircraft and floating barges mounting various antiaircraft cannon and guns. Bougainville was a major bastion of Japanese power and Tonolei Harbor and Empress Augustus Bay were the only two harbors to supply an estimated 45-60000 soldiers and naval personnel.

I describe this island and this harbor in some detail because we flew over that rotten place 8 times in my stay in the South Pacific. Every mission was terrifying and Hollywood could not possibly make a horror movie as scary as one of those missions. In addition to all the antiaircraft guns and cannon there were four Japanese air bases within support of the harbor.

To attack Tonolei, we would come into Bougainville from the south west and make land fall on or near Cape Friendship which was really inappropriately named after the Japs took over the island. It was easy to see if you were in the right position because there was a large lake – Lake Lehala to the north east and large mountains to the north west. The mountains were always covered in cloud cover that basically started in the trees and went up to 10,000 feet. We could see through the patchy stuff but in some attacks the cloud cover was so thick I might as well have been in that hateful Link Trainer again. We'd come down through the clouds over the pass and once over the harbor drop down as close to sea level as possible. Then it was shoot up anything in the harbor, drop the bombs – admittedly on crabs sometimes and get the heck out of there. We never made two passes on the same mission at Tonolei – that was just asking to be shot down.

As I said, Tonolei was a slash in the side of a mountain. The sides were steep and the harbor was narrow and the Japs had way too much antiaircraft weapons and there was no shortage of antiaircraft ammo. Their Brass decided that the harbor had to be protected and they had to make a stand on this island, so they were rather stingy with us about flying over there.

The harbor was protected by two airbases Kara and Kahili airfields though our intelligence only knew of Kahili. We found the second airbase by accident the hard way. Between the two bases there were easily a 100 planes on any given day available for intercept or fighter defense. If it was a big push, planes from the two northern bases were shipped down to support as well. As this was a joint Japanese effort we ran into both Japanese Army and Naval aircraft.

The US Brass had some sort of fixation about that place but I never saw anything of consequence in there, couple of times we caught some barges in there and once or twice a couple of destroyer escorts or corvettes but no big ships and never did see any cargo ships in Tonolei. I had eight missions in Tonolei. All our leaders always went in from the top and came out the bottom, flying over the gap to the east over the saddle to the harbor's north east and then flying westerly exiting out the mouth of the bay. I had trouble with that because we would have to go close to a Jap strip near Kahili on the exit route. It was grass and not easy to see, but there was always a lot of automatic weapons and anti-aircraft cannons near it, not to mention the Jap fighters that could launch at a moment's notice.

The attack path did make sense; on a gun run it is hard enough to shoot cannon and machineguns as well as drop bombs on ships in a harbor or attack harbor defenses or the harbor mechanisms and supplies and fly out the open end of the bay to the sea. It would be significantly more horrifying shooting up all that stuff and dodging all that flack and antiaircraft fire AND climbing up the face of a mountain to escape.

The most dangerous hit I took was at the Kahili airfield. The Japs had gone to the blanket barrage system of firing at attacking aircraft. They fused weapons at 8,000 – 10,000 feet, another set at 10,000 – 12,000 feet and the last barrage grouping at 12,000 – 14,000 feet. Ammunition would be fused to concentrate at those levels and be able to reach anything flying at those levels. Of course one of the dangers in flying through flak barrages is not only must the pilot and plane endure the explosions of the flack artillery, but the falling shrapnel from barrages above are just as dangerous as the explosions

At that time our bombing raids were huge. One day we were brought in at 14,000 feet and I was spaced behind squadron leader Collins. We were going fast so we wouldn't be exposed longer than necessary and we were not flying straight or at the same altitude making random height and direction changes as we approached. It really was most likely a waste of gas – a hit by flack artillery is completely accidental no matter how much they aim at you, but it did make us feel better in that we were doing something.

I always hunched as much as possible, close behind the bulletproof glass, as I could get. That put my face as close to the windscreen as possible.

A big shell went off close to my right wing tip. Only one piece of shrapnel hit the ship. A big piece cut straight across the fuselage just in front of my windshield slicing the maintenance access panel for the canon in half. The piece facing the slipstream snapped up straight in front of my face and as I was probably going close to 350 miles an hour the boom could be heard for miles.

The hit was only a few inches in front of my face. The damage was actually minor and the maintenance folks had the plane repaired before the next mission but the fear factor on that hit was near fatal – and there is a somewhat famous joke about the color of trousers I was wearing after that hit and Collins mentioned something about screaming like a girl. After I found I wasn't blown up I regained composure and dropped my 500 pounder right next to Collins' bomb. When the squadron returned I excused myself from the ready line and cleaned up. When I got back the access panels had been replaced and the cowling had been repaired.

One time the second flight element leader, a Captain Longhorn, was taking a six ship flight in for a search and strafe. I was along for the ride as the good Captain was a newbie to the area and needed an old head to guide him through. I'd been on the island about six - eight weeks and therefore I was an old head. The weather was poor and the notch that we used was in total cloud cover. He started to circle trying to find out how to get in to the target from Cape Friendship and was actually debating whether or not to hit the harbor from the sea. I convinced him that was a no go in evidently a loud and excited enough voice that he changed his mind. I rarely yelled at senior officers unless they tried to kill me and then I was quite vociferous in my response to a suicidal attack plan. He still couldn't see our normal attack point and while searching for the notch he was at a low altitude and working right over the Jap field at Kahili.

One thing I knew and that was Jap airfields have a lot of automatic weapons around them. They also have lots of cannon and antiaircraft batteries as well, not to mention fighter aircraft. We later found out that Kahili was not the only Jap strip on the island and that a second base was at Kara which could and frequently did provide support for Kahili. I finally yelled at him saying he was going to get somebody killed if he didn't get out of here. He said he didn't know how to get into the bay.

I think I had been through there four times before, so I told him to follow me into the cut. I whipped over and dove into the clouds. I called the guys and told them to stay right behind me because there were rocks in the clouds. In my mind, the danger of hitting the mountains was far less than all those Japs squirting thousands of bullets at us. And that was exactly what they were doing.

When you dive into a target you may, at times, see a flash from a gun but you will never see the bullets. If however you glance behind you, you can see tracers after they have passed you. That is a very sobering sight, especially when it looks like a solid orange line. It is especially sobering when you know that there are about four hard bullets in between each tracer you can see. It has been my misfortune to have seen thousands of tracers.

On that particular mission when I broke out below the cloud cover I swung hard left. The Japs had a four barrel, 40 mm anti-aircraft piece in a hole up on the side of the mountain. It was a good location because anyone coming in, as we did, wasn't likely to see it in time to turn into it. Also it was placed high on the mountain side and in effect had a level or even a downward firing solution on the attacking aircraft.

The strange part is that I had seen that gun 3 times before. It seems that someone had determined that gun was positioned at the exact place it needed to be so no matter how many times we knocked it out they put the gun back in the exact same location. My first attack on the bay it took me by surprise and I had to call a warning to the other folks in my flight. The second time we attacked I was looking for it and filled the position with machinegun and cannon fire. After my second mission in there I knew the Japs would always put it right back in the same place so I was ready for the turn in this mission.

I can see if someone higher up has determined the gun had to go into that position but they could have covered it with a secondary gun because when you're flying into the harbor, 40mm cannon shells are the last thing you want to see so you eliminate that threat first. In all the missions I ran in there, not one time did they move that gun or cover it with a secondary weapon. I know the gun was replaced several times as I personally shot it up but each replacement went in the same gun pit.

They were waiting but so was I. I let go with .50 and .30 caliber weapons at about a thousand yards which I'm sure upset those people. They certainly didn't have time to get on me. At five hundred yards I fired the cannon and put three rounds into the hole with the gun and the gunners. That time the gun was knocked completely out of the hole. At that point I had to reef in very hard to escape hitting the mountain above the gun pit.

The next plane in line didn't have to fly though the barrage from that gun but there were several more positions waiting for us. The cure was to get low and stay low. Some Jap officer had decided the optimum barrage effect should be at 4000 feet elevation and the secondary at 8000 feet, we had to come into the pass in that window but once cleared dropped down as low as possible. We stayed very low because many of their gunners couldn't shoot much of the time because their rounds would easily carry across the bay and endanger their own men.

As strange as it may seem there were no ships in the bay, despite what our intelligence briefing had said. Later in life I got real resentful of intelligence. I got down close to the water and was just wasting ammo on Jap latrines that hung out over the water. We'd come all this way I was going to shoot up something. A Jap soldier was hiding in front of me and suddenly jumped up throwing his rifle at my plane. I couldn't react and it was too late for me to depress or I'd hit the ground. In the fraction of seconds that he had he swung his rifle from between his knees straight up in front of me. I'm positive the prop blades went one on each side of the rifle.

I was kind of perturbed at that young fellow because if that 26 dollar rifle had hit my prop there is a good chance my 42,000 dollar airplane would have been splattered all over the cliffs and my next of kin would get my 10,000 insurance policy. The economics on the deal just did not work out in the USA's favor. I would have loved to turn around and discuss that event with the soldier but we had one rule on a search and strafe, get in, get hits, get out. I hit the combat boost and launched out the bay towards the sea and our rally point.

The only satisfaction I had at that time was I knew the Jap army was as tough on their folks for losing their rifles as the US army was on our guys. I have always thought a Jap Sergeant screaming at that guy was probably worse than what I could do with my cannon and machineguns. He probably thought twice before throwing another rifle at a strafing airplane and scaring the crap out of pilots like me.

On another attack on Tonolei there was a very young man flying in the second section. He just turned 19 and I have no idea how got in the Air Corps at such a tender age. He would have had to have passed the aptitude test when he was 17 which was possible, just not likely. He followed me on the gun run but while going down the left side of the bay he suddenly decided to cross over to the opposite side.

All the Japs were lined along the sides of the bay, so any plane would be passing in front or over them. Any plane crossing the bay lost the advantage of the forward motion he had in the attack.

We came roaring out of that pass at full firewall. That would put us at over 400 MPH in the dive, granted we slowed for accurate firing so assume we are making 300 miles an hour, which makes a terribly hard target to hit. Lead is real hard especially for the ground mounted flack. Enemy gunners cannot shoot where they see the plane, they had to shoot where the plane was going to be when the bullets reached the position of the plane and that was not an easy task. Add a constant shifting by the pilot in altitude and attitude and any hits by flak were more accident than aimed. In that situation I think most gunners would just spray in front and hope the plane would catch a hit or two as he passed through. That situation is particularly true where the range is very short, as it was at Tonolei.

To turn across the bay made the aircraft become what gunners call a 'sitter'. Aiming becomes much more simple in that there is no lead to figure, the plane is either coming directly at you or passing away from you, with high powered high muzzle velocity anti-aircraft munitions being fired, in many respects the target seems to be standing still. Then the gunner is only concerned with elevation. His chances of getting a hit are greatly improved.

The kid placed himself in the worst position he could and took several hits. His luck held and all the hits were up front and almost straight down. He must have tried to make a sharp turn. That was likely why they missed the engine and the inter cooler, not to mention the pilot. He got back to home plate ok but was absolutely hysterical. He bounced the plane on landing and was a total wreck. He never flew again and was sent home to the States.

Many of us took hits of one sort or another but weren't affected like that kid. He wasn't alone though we had two other men relieved with combat fatigue. I had some experience with another man not of our squadron. Those men became very dangerous.

Flying conditions were either totally hectic, flying 4-7 missions per day, basically living in the cockpit with a rare inconvenient break for the privy, followed by more flying; or it was getting bombed or shelled, flying 4-7 missions a day (same privy requirements) or it was getting bombed or shelled or sniped at and flying 4-7 missions a day with small increments of a break for the privy. Or it rained and we did nothing.

It would rain so hard that you literally couldn't see your hand in front of your face and that would last for hours. The camp was knee deep in water; we'd take off our flying shoes and wear them around our neck, roll up our trousers, and wade barefoot through the camp. Then there would be a small break in the rain which was just long enough to heat the place up to an oven, followed by rain so heavy you couldn't see your hand in front of your face.

By far the worst flying was being bombed or shelled or sniped and flying 4-7 missions a day with small increments of a break for the privy - in the rain. It either rained so hard we were grounded and were bored out of our mind; or it rained enough that we could fly and were scared out of our shorts. The rain made it all dangerous.

It was hard to walk from the Ops hut to the privy let alone the flight line. It was downright terrifying taking off in a mass of spray and prop wash, muddy water splattering the canopy. If take off was hard, rain played total havoc on a plane trying to land a tricycle configuration at the second fastest landing speed of any fighter in any air force in the world. Only the German jet the ME262 had a faster landing speed and that one could only be operated out of improved airbases.

The P39 Airacobra had a landing speed of between 95 - 110 miles per hour with a tricycle landing gear. Land three points with one of them being on the nose was a difficult process– landing on a muddy strip; Marston mats covered in mud and soaked in rain water – despite being an elevated surface was often deadly.

Landing in a three point configuration was so unique at the time that the training manuals made special notes concerning how to land. The following is from the P39 Airacobra Operating Instructions:

"Forget that the ship has a tricycle type landing gear and make a normal type landing. This type landing should be one where the nose of the airplane is well up and the main wheels touch the ground before the nose wheel. (In other words a landing attitude equivalent to that with a conventional gear.) The typical landing will result in a landing speed between 95 – 110 mph. Once the main wheels touch the ground, the plane will without any help from the pilot nose down until the nose wheel is on the ground. There will be no tendency whatsoever for the airplane to ground loop or bounce."

I was returning from a run where we found zero enemy indication. (That intelligence thing I keep harping on). My flight of 4 ended up dropping our bombs in the sea because no one was allowed to land with ordinance still hanging on their shackles unless it was a damaged bird or some kind of emergency. I stress we had no enemy contact and the planes were in good operating order. Because the strip was so wet, the only way to approach was to land short, let the bird roll out the entire length of the strip to bleed off ground speed, and at the far end of the strip, touch the brakes.

I came in at just over stall speed and despite the rain saw the beginning of the strip through my side window. I was at full flap with the wing indicator showing two thirds red and one third yellow. I fully wished there was an even wider flap indicator but that setting gave me as much flap as I could get. I slipped over and touched down as close to the end of the strip as I possibly could. I threw the Prop Pitch Control lever to full and cut the engine rpms to barely turning over. I let it roll out for what seemed like forever full flaps and the engine throttled down to just barely over idle. The plane slowly slowed and I was able to touch my brakes eventually stopping short of the run off for the strip. Having done this, I applied power and pulled my plane off the strip and watched the rest of my flight land.

My number 2 touched down at nearly the exact spot I did, rolled out and touched the brakes before dumping enough speed. He skidded to the right, slid to the left and fell off the runway crushing his landing gear and 3 bladed prop. He also managed to bash his head into the sight reticle and broke not only his skull but the mounting for the gun sight. He walked away from the crash but the plane needed serious maintenance before it was going to fly again.

Number 3 didn't stand a chance, he came in long and rather than apply combat power and attempt to pull up, he touched down and rolled out. By the time he realized his mistake he'd lost too much speed to actually take off again. He slammed on the brakes, skidded into a slide and ended up rolling the plane on its left wing. He walked away but that was another plane in the spares bin.

I had hopes for number 4 but he was a rookie as I recall and the P39 could be unforgiving. He stalled out and bounced on the strip, attempted to pull more power, and slammed in to the strip again and the spray of the muddy water coated his canopy and pretty much blinded him. From that moment on he was just a passenger along for the ride trying to hold on as the plane skidded off the runway and splashed into a pond of rain water. His bird was actually the least damaged in that only the lead landing gear and the prop needed to be replaced – after the plane was fished out of the pond.

Four planes, no combat action, zero damage, all in perfect operating condition and two of the four needed depot level repair and the third was a complete write off. Our maintenance guys were phenomenal – they had the pond plane in a flying condition - what we called up – before dinner and they had the missing wing plane up before midnight – though the plane used the wing from a wreck that had been pushed to the side of the strip.

I had been on the island for 6 weeks and Major Hecht did a horrible thing – he made me a permanent flight leader. I had filled that role when Collins was out and when they found out I had previously been a Corporal it just seemed I naturally fell into these "command" slots. Anyway we got a passel of new guys and I was assigned to take several of them to the Shortland Islands for their Baptism of Fire.

In order for this to make sense we have to delve into some quick history. Operation Cartwheel was going to be kicked off in June of

1943, of course I knew nothing of it; the brass was hesitant to brief Second Lieutenants in their rationale and planning for winning the war. However in preparation for that operation, the Army made an unopposed landing on the Russell Islands about 60 miles north west of Henderson Field in Guadalcanal on February 21 1943. We routinely worked out of Henderson and one of the three fighter strips on the Russell Islands, the places were basically interchangeable although serious maintenance efforts still needed to be conducted at Henderson. If we were not directed to the Russell Island air strips we normal based out of Henderson.

We were flying from the Russell Islands at that time. The few times I went to Shortland I was always amazed as it was devoid of any foliage, at least any that I could see. We came in over the beach at an altitude just above the highest terrain feature I could see roughly 300 feet.

Right on a bald knob in front of us a Jap was walking as if he had not a care in the world. He stood there looking at me as if I was flying a spaceship from outer space. He displayed no fear simply an overwhelming curiosity, which upon reflection here I was a US pilot from around the other side of the globe flying a plane completely different from his experience and I can understand how he just might think me from a distant planet.

He was tall, he was fully dressed wearing his shirt unbuttoned at the neck and had one of those soft Japanese hats with the cloth hanging from the rear of the hat. He wore mid-calf boots and looked the consummate professional. He was not an officer that I could see in that he did not have a pistol or a sword. He leaned on his rifle and watched me fly by. I studied him as he watched me and we both had one of those rare moments of live and let live. I had literally no animosity towards him and he took no aggressive action against me. He apparently just wanted to watch me fly. I nodded at him and he acknowledged the courtesy.

I ignored him looking for some value targets until I heard some guns going off behind my ship. The rookies in my flight barreled in and unloaded on that unfortunate. I thought they were going to run into each other trying to get a shot at the man. I was livid screaming into the mike for them to break off and cease firing but if they heard me they pretty much ignored me. There is a lot of things that happen in battle with faulty communications but the one where the junior pilot goes "KSKSKKKKKKKSSSTTT can't hear you" end up most times getting someone killed. Events like that usually end up with counseling sessions behind the nearest hanger. I actually saw one flight leader draw his pistol and fully believe he would have shot the wayward pilot if not restrained by his ground crew.

I had 6-8 weeks in theater, all that new stuff that I took such copious notes on was routine for me now, although I still wrote more than the comm frequency on my hand. Those baby fresh punk kids were going to do what I said when I said it or there was going to be some serious butt chewing. Not to mention that they had completely ignored my formation brief and that we now had no one in a top cover position, they had all come down to shoot at the Jap. I blasted them for a good bit and I had some hard things to say to those fellows when we got back.

When I finally got control of my wayward fledglings and we strafed along the beaches doing little or nothing, they needed the gun practice as evidenced by their lack luster performance with the man on the knoll. The Japs were very clever at hiding things with camouflage so we could in theory be hitting stuff that was well hidden but in fact I was just letting the guys fire their guns. If they hit the island I couldn't prove it.

I popped over a small ridge and stumbled on a trench. I came on it from the end and that is why I could see it. There were quite a few men in it and they were all getting their weapons. I got my sight on the trench and fired a quick burst from end to end of the trench. I bellowed for the rest of my element to fall into column which is a flight formation called line astern, and begin their runs on the trench east to west. I was hard on the rudder to guide the new guys into the attack and their efforts were more than pathetic. I think some of them hit the island but I would not put any money on it.

I was still fuming at their poor marksmanship, and their previous performance in flight and fire discipline and I ranted and raved at these folks using some language my mother never heard come out of my lips. This was an opportunity to hit a legitimate target and cause some damage to the Japanese war effort and my flight was acting like a bunch of school girls. I reefed hard across the front of the trench and began another run down the length of the trench which I would estimate to be 3-400 yards long. I was livid and was disregarding the prime directive as the star trek fans would say. We always hit and ran, this was my second run and the Japs knew from where I was coming.

What I didn't see was a rig the Japs had set up. It was a wagon wheel with its axle buried in the ground and a 12.7mm (.50 calibers) mounted on it. There were two men standing on that jury rig manning the gun and they had to be crazy to man that weapon facing my plane but they stayed on that wagon wheel and fired at me. They were right on me and I took several hits in the right wing. I hit them with everything I had - 37mm cannon, .50 and .30 caliber machineguns and several harsh words. I got a quick glimpse as I flashed by and that contraption was nothing but smoking dust when I passed.

But I knew I had been hit and I was desperate to get back over the water because I didn't know how bad the hits were. I called my flight over to our rally point and told them to break off, we had enough baptism and it was time to get back before anyone did something really stupid like get killed on my watch.

I was about to further my education again. I made the gentlest turn I could so as not to put unnecessary stress on the wounded wing. I didn't climb or maneuver, I was going to get out over the water and head directly home after I got one of the rookie pilots to give me a look see to ensure I could get home. I crossed the beach about 30 feet high and learned all there was to know about Water Canons in that moment.

A slug of water shot up about 10 feet off the right wing and in rapid succession three others went up to my left, making a line from the one beside me. The water slugs were about 12 inches thick I'd guess and I'd guess ten to twelve feet long and easily hit an altitude of nearly 100 feet. The operator must have had switches for each segment of four water cannons. I had never even heard of a water canon before. I called my flight and told them to stay away from the beach and swing wide to the ocean as I could not figure how I was going to explain this to the CO if I lost a plane to a high powered squirt gun.

I know I cannot convince some that the Japs actually used these water cannons. The same nation that thought it was a strategically sound decision to build helium balloons with mini incendiary bombs as a legitimate method of bringing America to its knees by setting all the forests in the Western States afire possibly would not see anything wrong with putting water cannons on a beach to shoot down low flying aircraft. I have seen many ship borne water cannons on tugs and firefighting vessels and am constantly reminded of that beach at the Shortlands.

My problem now was to decide what was best to try. I eased up to about 300 feet and had my wingman slide underneath for a look. I knew several of the hits were in my .30 caliber ammo trays because some ammo had been driven through the top skin of the wing.

I really should have thought this through better, having a rookie give a battle damage report was not the brightest thing I have ever done. He panicked and said a place about two feet square was all torn up and I had to get out now before the wing fell off. He suggested that I try to get a bit more altitude and jump. I reminded him of the Army Air Corps dictum which states "It is not a good idea to bail out over an area you have just bombed or strafed."

I decided to get a bit higher and just hang on. I was afraid to slow down or change anything for that matter, because a change in attitude might take the wing off. At 50 miles out I started to work the throttle back and by the time I crossed the end of the runway was slow enough to put the bird down. The manual says the indicated air speed cannot be greater than 125 MPH for landing gear deployment and as soon as I hit that I deployed. When the gear dropped my number 2 started yelling that the tire was blown off and all I had was the strut and the wheel. I did have the sense to tell him there are just some things people trying to make an emergency landing in a shot up bird just did not need to know when they are coming in and can do nothing about it.

I was indicating 120 MPH and chopped to 100 MPH as quickly as I could. The slower I got the further the wing twisted. The right tire had been hit and was blown off which made the right tip look even worse when I got on the ground. It was not a fun landing that day but the wing held and it was one from which I managed to walk away.

That night the maintenance team put a different wing on my bird as a replacement for the one that was shot up. It wasn't the correct wing for this model but it fit the airplane. I was told it was longer than what was supposed to go on this ship but the factory rep said it wouldn't hurt anything because they swapped them frequently in their test work. The mechanics found that the main wing spar was split for several feet and this did nothing for my facial color, I went just a slightly paler shade than pure white and when I thought how close that wing was to falling off in the sky I turned a dull green and sought the nearest tree.

When I awoke the next morning my ship was ready to fly. I could not believe it as after I got down I thought the only good thing about that mission was I would have a couple of days off while they put my ship back in commission. Or I thought, I could get a trip back to New Caledonia and get to pick a new plane. Either way I was thinking I had some time off coming. Sometimes our maintenance guys were simply too good.

That replacement wing never gave me any problems. I never felt more or less lift or drag on that side and if anything the wing made the plane more stable in level flight. One small strange thing resulted from that flight, my compass never worked correctly again, but it never happened with a mechanic standing by to fix it. It only started to act up when I was in the air trying to make some life or death decision on which way I should go. The mechanics traded out that compass several times to keep me from whining but each replacement had the same non-working characteristics once the plane was out of sight of the mechanics. None of which could be demonstrated to the mechanics, who probably thought I was a loon.

As for my wayward flight, I went over to Collins' tent who was acting for Major Hecht and requested all three of those newbies be assigned to my new element. Collins looked at me funny for a bit and then nodded the ok. From that day on at least three planes flew in formation and learned fire discipline and fire control. I had blasted them after my landing, and the following morning I ripped them yet again. That mess on the knoll was never repeated.

There was a mission I liked and I caught several of them. Every once in a while a Navy task force would come by going someplace and when they were passing the island we would fly close cover. When this support mission was posted on the daily board I always signed my element up. I also always got first crack at those missions because I was permanent dawn patrol, thus I always got to the daily mission board first.

I never knew how fast the big battleships could go but it must have been a bunch. They never seemed to take their time but were always going like gang busters. Those battleships were under the water at least half the time. It was a sight to see which I'll never forget. Both my brothers were in the Navy and there was a strong naval tradition in my family – after all my grandfather sank a clipper ship in the blizzard of 1886. His parting comment being something to the effect that there was no storm that could sink a Case. I said it was a strong naval tradition I never said it was a glowing tradition...

I had another of those missions, but over a convoy that was going much slower. Transports that were to participate in landing operations brought barrage balloons with them. Some were inflated and on short tethers for the duration of their travel. Suddenly a barrage balloon ripped up just in front of me. It almost hit me and all I could think of was a cable was hanging down and what kind of damage that steel cable would do to my spinning prop.

Once again I thought about the economics of this deal and how a 1200 dollar barrage balloon taking out a 42,000 dollar plane and an expensive pilot was just not a fair trade or in the best interests of the government. Somehow that balloon missed my plane and the reason it was loose was because there were no cables. Once again I thought of the airline hostess and the power of prayer.

There were another small group of flyers we worked with who don't seem to get much attention from anybody. They were the Dumbos. These were the big twin engine amphibians – PBY Catalina - that the Navy stationed all over the theater. All of these men that I met were young and they displayed unheard of bravery which was not just 'beyond the call of duty' but far beyond the call of duty. These kids would bring those planes into live fire areas and pick up a downed airman in the sea and it didn't matter if he was Navy, Marine, or Army Air Forces they were right there. If a plane went down near an island they routinely took fire while fishing out the downed pilot and would place the airplane between the gunners on the beach and the downed pilot.

One morning I think every fighter aircraft in theater was up. I have no idea why but Army, Navy, and Marines were up and were going to demonstrate to the empire of Japan why it was not a good idea to pick a fight with the US. I had barely broke ground when I heard a 'may-day' from a guy up at Bougainville saying he was going down off the beach at Kieta. Another from a New Zealand guy saying he had 20 Japs surrounded at Khahili and he could use some help. Two B-25s were down and before we got to the area it was a downright nasty knife fight. The Japs wanted to dance and the US forces were accepting the invitation.

Now the Dumbos were lifesaving crews. They would land in the sea to pick up downed airmen. It didn't matter what kind of sea, they would go down and get the guys overloading the plane if necessary to the point of they couldn't get off again. A second Dumbo would land, take off some of the downed crews and then both planes would take off. I saw one Dumbo that had been hit rescuing a downed pilot and the crew "abandoned ship" when a second Dumbo came in to evacuate the damaged plane.

My entire squadron was in the air and Hecht took us up high. We could hear most of the battle because everybody was on one control frequency it seemed. Planes were falling left and right and we made a pass at some Jap formation of ancient Nates that really should have not been in theater. Jap Army Oscars and Navy Zeros were flying top cover and they were mixing it up with the P39 boys and the Marine F4Fs.

I heard a P38 go down and one of the B25's went down as well. There was already one crew from a 25 in the water when the Dumbo came in flying right above the sea. They went after the P-38 guy and got him. Then they got the B-25 crew that had been in the water. Without taking off they taxied to pick up another downed pilot and then got the crew from the second B25.

That Dumbo had a full load but the call came in that a Marine was belly landing an F4 into the drink and the Dumbo pilot had to go to the Shortlands to get him. In the process his plane got hit and picked up some holes in the nose section of boat. He couldn't take off so he put the healthy bodies he had just rescued on the back straddling the fuselage to try and raise the nose of the plane. He picked up the Marine and then he taxied several miles away from the Shortlands to await rescue himself.

My flight got to cover the last part of the rescue as a second Dumbo landed and pulled all 12 rescued men and the 4 man crew off into their ship. After they were air borne we had to make gun runs on the ship to sink it and it was like shooting a cavalry horse that had broken its leg. The crew and the plane were more than heroic

Another time we were diverted from something else because we had a twelve ship formation. There was a downed pilot close in at Shortland and we were flying top cover. We were doing the escort and I found the guy in the water. He was much too close to the beach and the Japs knew he was there. The Dumbo made his approach and the Japs were shooting at the plane with what must have been mortars. If they were shooting anti-aircraft weapons it would have been no contest but the mortars were not that accurate.

Despite several gun runs by our ships the mortars kept coming in at the rescue plane. They were close and I'm sure shrapnel was hitting the flying boat. That kid stayed until he had the man out of the water and then amongst a hail of fire took off right in front of the Japs.

Those men did those missions over and over again but I have never heard of even one word of praise for that service.

I found four downed flyers total, at different times and the Dumbos always came and got them all. One was a nineteen year old class mate of mine. He didn't come down with us because he had lied about his age and couldn't go to combat until his next birthday. He got shot down on his first mission.

I had another sad event coming back from Buka where I was siding a kid who had been hit. He struggled to keep the plane in the air but he was steadily losing altitude and finally decided it would be better to land in the sea with some control and power than crash into the sea. He landed the bird in the water close to the edge of a coral reef. He got in his raft and made it to the reef. Up to that point he had done everything exactly right but then he decided to get out of his raft and stand on the reef. He was standing on the coral in water about waist high on the edge close to deep water.

I had called for a Dumbo and was doing a slow orbit around the guy at fifteen hundred rpm to save gas. Suddenly a black shape slid up from the deep water. The kid never saw him and even in a power dive at combat boost I could not reach the scene in time. I guess I thought I'd make a gun run on the shark but it was all over too fast. It only took about two seconds. Outside the reef the sea was deep to untold depths and the shark took the downed pilot to the bottom.

One of the big misconceptions of the Pacific theater is that everyone thinks the main opponent in the air was the Japanese Zero, but they forget that aircraft was a naval weapon. The Zero got all the press both US and Japanese but it was not used by the Japanese Army Air Forces (JAAF).

The Japanese Army aircraft often times looked like Zeros in the case of the Oscar and Frank but did not have the Zero's performance or armament. Having read some specs for the JAAF, the major design consideration was the maneuverability of the plane. The Jap Brass wanted their Army fighters to be able to dogfight first and then they worried about speed, climbing ability, and armament. They never did worry about the pilot's survival so the planes had little to no armor plate and very primitive self-sealing tanks. Unlike the Zero which was heavily armed most of the JAAF planes had 2 or 4 machineguns and routinely these were 30 caliber.

And here I shall pontificate on the Japanese military and naval cooperation during the war. They were insane to the point of stupid. I know US Army folks will cheer for West Point when they play the Navy at Annapolis and the same can be said for the Navy even if the spectators don't like football or basketball they still cheer for their service team; but they won't try to slit each other's throat and they won't intentionally let another service get slaughtered so they can look good.

The Jap Navy hated the Jap Army almost as much as we did, and the feeling was mutual in the Army. Inter-service cooperation was almost non-existent with the Navy being forced to cover the Army's advances only by prime ministerial decree. Naval fighters provided their own security for their land based airbases and to guard their harbors, the Jap Army had something like 15 escort aircraft carriers to protect their convoys and troop movements because the Navy had something else on their plate. The Navy had the Zero and it was a good plane for its time, possibly great, the Army would have to make due with something else.

The US had a similar situation in that Naval aviation needed specific design requirements in order to survive a landing on a carrier that a land based plane did not - and naval planes needed a tail hook to keep the plane from rolling off the deck. That is understandable and in the case of the WW2 leadership can be easily excused, there was not a huge technical leap difference in aircraft design.

In fact in most navies of the time, the naval aircraft trailed their land based counterparts in performance because of the added weight to withstand a carrier landing. Given that there were slight advantages for the land based planes the F4F Wild Cat was comparable in performance to the P40 Warhawk, same for the F6 and F8 and the P47 and P51. They were of comparable technical advancement. Not so for the Zero– it completely outclassed nearly all the Japanese Army aircraft, yet the Army continued to fly underpowered, limited ranged, under armed, air planes (not that I am complaining).

When we did see a Zero we vacated the area, Zeroes were bad news with a capital B and the Navy pilots were a step above the JAAF pilots, as much as that pains me to write. We avoided those planes like the plague if they were in the air. If we caught them on the ground it was happy time for us because on the ground the Zero was as useless as a rock.

When Zeros or Oscars caught us we still had some advantages. We could not turn with them or climb with them but we could out dive them and in the case of the Nates and Oscars we could pull away in level flight as the P39 was significantly faster.

If the Japanese pilots made the mistake of getting in front of us we had the best advantage, better sighting equipment and more bullet throwers than they could bear. My P39 configuration was two 30 cal machineguns in the fuselage, two 50 cal machineguns in the wings and a 37 mm cannon in the nose. All of it geared to start putting hits on a plane at 1000 yards. Additionally the P39 could take a hit and keep flying, the Japanese planes other than the Tony couldn't; they tended to flame up as soon as they were hit, and as stated the Army planes were very lightly armed.

I don't want to make it sound like we were afraid of the Japs, I would joke and say we were terrified but truth be told we respected them and took them for what they were. Our planes were not the best planes to mix it up with them so we developed tactics that would give us a chance for success. They couldn't stay with us in a dive and we had better firepower. We used those two assets and knocked down a fair share of Jap planes. If we got confused and tried to turn with them; that was called a kill and some Jap got to paint an American flag on his tail if they did that sort of thing. Therefore we didn't dogfight. Hit and run, get back to altitude, then hit and run.

At this stage of the war, Japan still had a technical edge on our planes, they had more experienced pilots, especially the naval aviators, and they were still undefeated. I understand there was some aloofness by the European pilots comparing the German to Japanese air forces and the general thought was that the Jap planes were all garbage and flamed if you looked at them crosswise and the Jap pilots were second class pilots. That was not the opinion of the folks that had to fight them, they were one tough group at this time and they were used to winning.

On a flight back from a strike at Bali airfield one of the pilots had to jump in the water. He had hoped to ride the bird back to the Russells but when the engine seized he had to bail. By sheer chance we had come up on one of the big amphibians, one of the larger four engine Martins. Hecht called the plane on the rescue frequency and told the guy he had a pilot in the water and he wanted the man to land and pick the pilot up. The flying boat guy said he was heavily loaded with beer so he couldn't land.

For a moment there was dead silence on the frequency. Then Hecht said 'Mister if you don't go get my pilot you won't need any beer, I will shoot you down myself."

I can't guess how many cases of beer they threw out but it was a bunch. I don't know who owned the flying boat but I'll bet they could have killed us but we got our pilot back. We also had a couple of beers in celebration of his safe return and the Martin's landing at our base.

While I was having all this fun at the Canal, some of my other classmates were checked out in P-40 War Hawks and were shipped off to New Guinea. Dan David was in that group and joined a P-40 Squadron in New Guinea.

Another man had been a class captain named Harry Andrews from Fresno. He got into P38 Lightenings which everybody wanted, but at that time few got. Andrews was scheduled to go to Guadalcanal with a First Lieutenant Besby F Holmes. Holmes was one of the old timers who was chosen to go on that special mission to get Yamamoto. He was a spare on the 18 ship flight but when two of the Killer Team had to abort due to mechanical malfunction, Holmes and the second spare were put into the section.

As they attacked the Betty bomber with Yamamato, Holmes' drop tank release would not function and he had to abort. During the abort he finally got his tank to detach and found the second Betty bomber and attacked that one over the sea with his wingman in tow. They got Yamamato's second in command Vice Admiral Matome Ugaki and sent him into the sea. They each got a Zero of the escort flight and managed to get back to the base.

This day Holmes was leading the two ship flight and had the flight just below an overcast cloud cover. Without warning, two Zeros dropped down out of the overcast, directly in front of the 38s going in the same direction, completely unaware of the P38 flight. Holmes had several kills to his credit but Andrews hadn't even fired his guns.

Holms signaled Andrews to take one and he would get the other. Andrews' target was the lead Zero and Holmes would pick up the tailing Zero. Andrews got his guns turned on and fired at the lead Jap flaming the tailing Zero. He quickly adjusted to get on the lead Zero and got that one as well. Andrews' first flight in the combat zone and first time to trigger his guns came home with two confirmed kills, although he was only supposed to shoot at the one. It was always an embarrassment to him that he missed his target by easily 200 or so yards and it was pure luck the bullets he was shooting at the lead plane hit the trailing plane.

I had plenty of embarrassing moments myself. The pilots were always engaging in little scrambles with each other, usually after a dull escort or convoy mission. If you could get on your partner's tail and yell guns guns guns before they could get out of the line of fire – you were the winner. I mostly had good luck with these scrambles and actually had a reputation for wining more than I lost. We found our ground crews often exchanged money on who was going to win the scramble and I slipped a few bucks to my plane captain to see if I could enhance my fiscal position along with my reputation.

There was another man who I hadn't ever tangled with named Derr who had some successes with other men in the squadron. Just like two big guys on the block someone had to see who the hot shot was. The guys got together with Hecht and got him to send us up. I didn't like that because we always just got together over the base at the end of a mission and rat raced for a couple of minutes, it was never formal but just fun.

In this engagement we separated and then turned back toward each other. We would pass keeping the other man on the left. That would be the start of the contest. I'm sure the people on the ground got a show because we did every maneuver known to flying. We looped and turned and flipped and had the engine on combat boost to the firewall. I tried every maneuver I could think of including the World War I Immelman to get on Derr's tail. After what seemed like an hour or two but in reality was only 15 – 20 minutes Derr finally was gaining into position where it would end in a tight circle and I wouldn't be able to get out of it. It was like a constrictor snake, the man was doing something that I couldn't equal.

That was what the Jap planes could do to any American fighter. We could only put the nose down and slam everything to the firewall and run. That way we could keep him out of range. Hopefully. In this case Derr had me; if I turned my tail toward him to run he would just blow it off, just as a Jap would do if you let him get in range before you started to run. If I tried to loop or pull up, Derr would close the distance even faster because the P-39 just did not climb. He had the advantage and the rules of the rat race were you couldn't combat boost in a dive out of there so that ended the contest. Derr said guns thrice and I quit maneuvering. Turns out my plane captain had ended up putting almost all my season's winnings on this one flight, not only did I come in second in front of the entire base, I ended up a much poorer man as well.

One more note on the Jap planes. Turning away from him didn't mean you gave up. It was only another maneuver in the fight. If possible you led him away from his home base and mostly he would have to quit quickly because he would never have much gas. As soon as you had the room the P-39 would turn to him and even if he turned back again the 39 had the advantage in gun power. It would be a rare Jap who would go head to head with a P-39. Conversely rat racing a Zero was about as unhealthy as you will ever get.

We had a rather unpleasant situation with the P-39s. There were several squadrons of them in the 13th Air Force and news of poor performance and accidents got around all the time. Rumors and wild stories not to mention real incidents got exaggerated into full blown horror stories. Crews just didn't want to fly that plane.

One rumor that got started was that P39s above a certain production number had a flaw in the main spar and the wing would fall off. We had a man in the squadron who complained bitterly that there was something wrong with his plane whose production number just happened to be higher than that from the rumor. The Major sent me up to check it to see if I could find the trouble, if any. I wrung it out thoroughly and hard with negative results.

Still not satisfied, Major Hecht traded planes with the guy making the pilot satisfied. That lasted for several months and everyone pretty much forgot about the curse of the production number. Hecht scrambled one afternoon for an intercept of a Jap reconnaissance bird. His airplane came apart and he was killed. There was no apparent reason but his wing fell off.

Some of the morale problems came to us on official letter head with a maintenance memo. We had a man who was loved more than anybody else in the squadron named Baily and he tended to be just a bit pudgy. We called him Mother Baily because he was always ready to help or assist anybody who needed it.

In our squadron there was a little ritual that we did a couple of times a month. The commander would get everybody who could fly in the air and we would go up and get in trail. The Old Man would lead us through a routine of simple acrobatics and cloud hopping. I have seen it from the ground and it looks like fun to see the birds go through holes in the clouds. It was simply to entertain the people on the ground although the flight logs all called it training.

One day Hecht had us up and when we got down the engineering officer met Hecht and handed him a message which was called a red border letter. Red Borders were messages oddly enough with red and white bordering which called for instant compliance. He went down the line of planes and had to shake the horizontal stabilizer to see if he could detect any problem.

He got to Mother Baily's ship and hardly touched it and the stabilizer fell off. We had just come down from an acrobatic exercise and if that stabilizer had fallen off there was no possible way Baily could have survived. The metal was crystallized. A hard landing might have snapped crystallized metal.

Word was that morale in our squadron was low and that got to our General. He came to visit us but he was flying a nice shiny new P-38. He was a nice, personable man who I thought was sincere, but the morale was really low. One of the things he said was we would all be getting P-38s soon because they were phasing out in Europe. That did happen but was too late for me. In the mean time he stated he would have a spare P40 delivered to our squadron so some of the boys could at least play with that one.

That night we gave a party for the General. People came from all over the island. They always brought whatever liquor they had and the cooks were able to scrape up a fairly decent meal. As usual it rained and it was in torrents. An unusually large flight of Jap bombers unloaded on us causing the party to come apart in a hurry. I had built my trench close to the ops shack. I knew it would have a lot of water in it but that was the least of my worries.

I dove in on the fly and landed on another body. I must have hit hardest on his head because I drove it down in the mud and water. Air raids like we had didn't last long and we got out of the shelters such as they were. There was activity in a trench a few yards away and I knew somebody was hit. That turned out to be the staff intelligence officer who was a lawyer, advanced in age, and rather fat.

When we ran for the trenches that guy was slow and got there late.

He tried to pile in to the only one he could find and dove in. Most of the people at the party were strangers who didn't have any idea where to go. In the gentle fashion of soldiers in combat we called our pudgy lawyer 'Belly Tank'. When he fell on top of the other men, his rump stuck up a few inches. A sizable piece of shrapnel cut a slash all across his behind. The Medic's got him and the party was over.

Back in the Ops shack in the light I saw the guy I had jumped on was the General. I apologized and he said something like "if you had done it right Lieutenant you would have brought a couple more guys."

When he went back he sent us a P-40 that had been through the Depot and was in good shape. It was for all the 'X' P-40 pilots to play with for relaxation. It did raise morale and we had contests and lotteries to see who got to fly the P-40 that day. I'm not sure that solved the problem. Most people preferred the P-40 because of the terrible reputation the P-39 but the 39 was easier to fly.

One of the guys went to Auckland, N.Z. for R&R and while he was there he bought a baby Boston Bull Dog which he brought back to the squad bay. The guys made a fuss over the little beast, feeding him tidbits from the mess and basically rough housing with him all day long if there was no mission. He would wander around with the men and one of the pilots actually took him up on a hop. During mission briefs he would follow us to the ops hut and probably paid more attention to the intelligence brief than we did. One day he was missing so people went out to find him. He had fallen into a bomb crater and drowned and that put a damper on anyone's morale.

A maintenance officer who was rotating back to the States when we arrived in the 67th Pursuit departed and left us a phonograph with one record. One side was a Glen Miller number (A String of Pearls) but the other side was a sentimental number. The singer was an Australian girl with a soft and very pretty voice named Joan Merele and the song was the very sentimental 'You Can't Hold a Memory in Your Arms.' We played that song literally a thousand times if not more. The machine was a hand winder and the only time that song was not playing in the background was when someone was winding the phonograph. Someone went on R&R to Australia and got a couple more records but I cannot think of a time that we were not playing that song.

We got a second visit from the commander of our Group after he delivered the P-40. The General told us that a squadron posted at Port Moresby had lost most of their planes and that many of the pilots had been rescued but didn't have anything to fly. The General said Admiral Halsey wanted us to go down there and share aircraft with those folks as there was a definite need for land based aircraft to cover his ships. Availability of land based fighters was a very serious matter for the Navy so I guess that was what was involved here.

The last thing the General said was

"Now I want you to listen to me. I don't want any rat racing with Zeros or Oscars. We have a fighter with a limited capability. If you see them in a position of advantage; put the nose down and get the hell out of there.

The next time you see them maybe you will have the advantage and then make them pay."

I guess he thought we were still rookies; I know he thought of us as his boys and hated endorsing letters home saying we had been killed. We were loaded with 109 gallon belly tanks and all tanks were topped off before we took off for New Guinea. We flew right on the water all the way down. Hecht wouldn't waste a drop of gas climbing although it could possibly have been more fuel efficient flying higher but then jet streams were just being discovered in World War 2.

About half the way down we had to pass a group of islands and there were Japs there. They had listening devices we knew and Hecht swung us wide off shore far enough so the curve of the earth would shield us from their listening devices. Another trick we were ordered to do was fly the tanks dry. Here we were right down on the water. If the engine didn't get fuel immediately you would go in the ocean.

I don't know about the other guys but in my case when the fuel gage read close to empty I turned on the boost pump and put my hand on the tank selector and then memorized what tank I was going to go to. My engine only started to hesitate and I snapped the selector. I heard some men say their engines had coughed before catching which was a somewhat harrowing event to happen to your plane's motor 100 feet above the water. Still all our birds made it to New Guinea.

NEW GUINEA

30 May - 28 June 1943

We landed at Milne Bay intact at Air Strip 1 renamed Gurney to honor RAAF Squadron Leader C.R. Gurney, a pilot who was killed in the crash of a B-26 – yes one of the Clip Wings. Milne Bay is seldom mentioned in the history books but there was a fairly large battle when the Japs invaded and were defeated by the Aussies.

The Jap intelligence was horribly off - they thought the 3 allied air strips under construction were guarded by but three infantry companies. They landed 1,250 Japanese Marines called Kaigun Rikusentai and found there were 7,500 Australian and 1,400 US Army personnel at Milne Bay, of whom about 4,500 were infantry. The Japs reinforced getting a total of 2000 Marines and soldiers on the island but they were simply overwhelmed.

The battle raged from August 25, - September 7, 1942. It was the very first time the Japanese war machine was defeated and the myth of Japanese invincibility was destroyed. The Jap plan for the area was to retake Guadalcanal and then launch a reinvigorated attack on the Australians around Port Moresby. In the end, defeats at Buna and on Guadalcanal ruined their plans; but when we arrived, they still thought an offensive action on New Guinea was highly possible and in fact a distinct possibility. Therefore since they would in the vernacular "be right back" they never let up running bombing and strafing missions on the fields.

We were told Milne Bay had the heaviest rainfall in the world. I believe it. All our structures were bamboo and grass. How they kept the rain out I don't know but in the main they did. The air strip was Marston Mats - steel planks - on dirt which instantly turned into mud just like Guadalcanal. The strip was supposed to be 6,000 ft long but because of the Japanese attacks; was cut to 4,000 and put into operation. It had many bad depressions in it where water and mud collected and the unwary pilot might lose control of the ship on both landings and take offs.

We were directed to walk the air strip prior to a take-off to see where the latest sink hole had appeared in the Marston Mats and report the new holes to the ops O who reported to the base commandant. As he had limited equipment to maintain the strip once the Seabees had gone it was a somewhat futile effort.

The dirt settled in places and when we flew from that runway it was an uncomfortable operation. It was said that for every four ship formation we flew we lost at least one tire to the ragged runway.

One morning we were all called into Ops for a briefing. That meant something special was going to happen. Major Hecht got right to it.

"I don't like this fellows but this is the way it will be. General MacArthur is going to take some VIPs up the coast to look at something. He's going to take two Gooney Birds and load em up with his staff and commanding officers. We will have the close cover responsibilities and there will be others in mid range and top cover as well. The 38s will be high and sweep in front, we are close support. We will never leave those two planes. You all know MacArthur has to get back – he's critical to the war.

We will stay with those two transports until they get back. If we get bounced we stay with the transports, if we run out of ammunition we will ram. No one will leave for any reason. Those Gooney Birds will come back."

I had never heard of such orders before and I certainly didn't like this. I distinctly remember feeling a cold chill. Generals are important but the US does not demand suicide missions from their troops, at least I thought they didn't.

MacArthur took two DC-3s loaded with his Generals to the Ramu valley. He intended to drop troops in there and he wanted his Generals to know what was there. The mission wasn't long and we didn't see anything. The 38s got into it though because I saw five flamers come down, but nothing came our way. There is a phenomenon that pilots call a 'no sky.' There are absolutely no clouds or any other thing to make a reference and you cannot see any of the combat above. Aircraft up high, probably about 20,000 feet are fighting for their lives and cannot be viewed from below. Only the flamers coming down can be seen.

They put a new crew chief on my aircraft and for some reason I wasn't told. The man was from the States and fresh out of school. Since different pilots flew those planes each flight, the crew chief always made sure everything was positioned to 'off' after each flight. Here we flew the same ship all the time except for rare exceptions. My new man checked my cockpit and shut everything to off.

For several months I had everything where I wanted it so when I got in, in the gloom of the morning I never even looked at anything. I fired up and rolled out. We had Curtis electric props at that time. The kid had shut off the power to the prop and of course I didn't know it. Recall that comment about the people that came back from mission after mission using the checklists? I had gone slack and there was no excuse.

The ship barely got off the ground and I couldn't hold position. I was about to go in the water when I saw the rpm was up to 4,000. I pulled the control back with no effect before realizing what was wrong. I was able to put the throttle and prop control back before hitting the prop switch. Everything went to normal but I lost the formation so I went around and landed.

That would be with a full load of fuel and ammunition. I didn't like that. I was introduced to the kid and he was terribly upset. We coordinated and were ok forever after. It was a subtle reminder that I was the one responsible for my ship, my crew chief had a stake in it but I was the one betting my life on it. When Hecht and the flight returned he had a few words for me but was not as brutal as he could have been or possibly should have been. I later found out that when one of the spare pilots flew his plane they had changed all the settings on him as well and he had a similar occurrence. We did get a command refresher brief on checking out the aircraft.

With multiple squadrons using the same aircraft we had to come to some kind of joint agreement as to what was going to be standard operating procedure. Why I always flew the same aircraft and no one else shared it with me I do not know. There were a couple of us that had that privilege although we did sometimes have to fly other ships on missions when ours were in the hanger for repairs or servicing.

Another day I came in from a mission and landed. I had big trouble holding the bird straight and something was grossly wrong with my brakes. I wrote it up and was told the maintenance guy was repairing my nose wheel. I was curious so I walked out in the woods where he was working.

He showed me where a bullet had struck a piece of the stabilizing gear in the nose wheel strut. There wasn't any bullet hole in the skin of the ship so it had to be after the gear came down or before it went up. The kid thought it ricocheted off the gear but since the gear only deployed upon landing and take-off or while sitting on the hardstand. We reported it to Intelligence as they would want to know there was a possibility of somebody sniping on our island.

I was kneeling across from the kid while he was working. We were called for chow and I said "see you after chow."

He said: "I only take a half hour when I'm working." I said "ok" and left.

We got back together. After we resumed the positions we had, before we left, he kind of reached behind him to get something in his tool box. I saw something like a shadow move in the box and I yelled. He jumped back and we saw what somebody called a Rock Python.

The Snake turned out to be six or seven feet long. It was slender and had coiled tightly to get in the box. Collins said it would bite but wasn't poisonous but it could infect the area around the bite. Either way it scared the living daylights out of us and we beat a hasty retreat until we could arm ourselves with various weapons of mass destruction, I had a pipe of about 4 feet in length and the mechanic picked up an axe handle. Now suitably armed we attacked the maintenance area ready for battle but found no adversary.present. To be truthful we really didn't spend that much time trying to find the snake either. We picked up the tools and the wounded strut and moved off to a more open area that was more heavily trafficked.

It was about that time we were ordered to go over to Ward's Drome. That was where I met George Welch again. He was rather small and was a quiet man when he was not drinking at least as much as I knew of him.

Welch was credited with three kills and one damaged at Pearl Harbor. The senior brass wanted to nominate him for the Congressional Medal of Honor for his actions in getting the two planes in the air and then between him and his wingman knocking down 5 Jap planes and damaging one. The recommendation was denied by the lower echelon staff in that Welch took off without permission. As insane as that sounds that is true and his CMH was downgraded to the Distinguished Service Cross – the second highest medal awarded by the Air Corps.

After Pearl Harbor and a stint with the war bond drive, George returned to combat with the 36th Fighter Squadron 8th Fighter Group New Guinea where they flew P-39s. George did not like the P39 – when asked what was good about it his response was that it had 1,200 lbs of Allison armor plate. He constantly hounded his command as to when they were going to transition out of P-39s to P-38s and the response "when we run out of P-39's" did not set well with him. He finally did transfer to P-38 Lightenings and racked up 9 more kills for a total of 16 before he was medically retired for Malaria. Something strange about George was that he never came back with just one kill – when he got a kill it was always multiple kills.

In our brief service together I liked the man. My first impression of him from Sydney was not the man I learned to respect. I was assigned to fly his wing on our first mission and that came up immediately.

A coast watcher called in with a report of 16 Nakajima 97s flying low on the other side of the Owen Stanley Mountains. That was the softest target we could possibly find. They were flying low so the radar couldn't see them but we had a general idea of where they were. We scrambled our ships and takeoff was hectic. George kept climbing and soon started pointing at me. I didn't have any idea what he meant but about that time I started to lose power. I started to check the cockpit and immediately saw I was still in full rich. I guess I was excited.

I felt like an idiot and I'm quite sure George felt the same way about me. He would have seen black smoke coming from my stacks. With the engine behind me I couldn't see my plane belching more smoke than that old steam locomotive.

We had been ordered to maintain radio silence. We all were supposed to have grid charts with us but George forgot his. If I was going to make excuses, I'd say it was understandable since he was flying a strange plane and it was not set up the way he would have had his plane set up if we were not sharing planes. We scrambled so there was a ton of excitement to get into the air, bottom line we should have been using those checklist

George was making all kinds of gestures to me and I didn't have any idea what he was talking about. The sum of that was we never got where we were supposed to be. I was the junior pilot I followed George, George didn't have his grid chart so he didn't know where to go. He indicated I should lead but I didn't have a working compass in my plane (perhaps why I always got the same plane) so I had no idea what direction the grid was at. I had the chart but no azimuth or bearing because my compass was pulled for maintenance and George had a working compass which could give us azimuth and bearing but didn't know where to go.

It was a mess and when George motioned me to break radio silence by holding his helmet in the air, I didn't have the proper frequency. I tried calling him on rescue 1 but we could not communicate. We were flying wing tip to wing tip and could not communicate. There was nothing left to do but return to base. Had we found those ancient crates we both would have been double aces. The Japs had no business putting planes that wouldn't qualify for training aircraft in that kind of position.

One admin note here – my son looked upon me as crazy when I mentioned that "non-operational" aircraft were constantly pulled off the line to run missions. A plane with no compass was an issue but someone in the flight would have a compass so we could make due until a new compass could be installed. Radios going out were an everyday occurrence and oft time had that works on the ground not in the air syndrome or works in Admin use but can't function in combat. Our planes were the hottest things in existence at the time cruising at 330

MPH, but the bottom line was it was just 330 MPH - we could fly closer than modern jets and we had extensive hand signals.

Morris Hecht was furious and upon reflection, Morris Hecht was furious quite a bit back then. Guess it comes with the job of Squadron Commander. The share system never worked and in a short time we were ordered back to Milne Bay. From Milne we flew many missions to the coastal fields and bombed many of them.

About this time we got a call from radar and they said they had a bogy to the north of us. It was near dark and they wanted to know if we wanted to take a look at it. Collins and I were still at New Guinea and he said we would. We went fast because it was getting dark and we had to go almost a hundred miles. The radar guy said we were right on the Bogy but we couldn't see him.

I thought maybe we were a bit too high which would have us looking down into the gloom. I dropped down about a thousand feet and looking up saw the Bogy in the twilight. Collins dropped down and I could direct him until he saw the aircraft. It was a P-38 running on one engine. The pilot turned out to be a green, new man and he was headed toward Lima, South America.

He had been shot up and when the engine quit he lost power to his compass and was lost. Radio was gone too. I believe the instruments ran on power from a 400 cycle generator. No engine. No generator.

We got him back to the bay and he landed ok. One of the small bullets, a 7.62 maybe, hit the crash strut that sloped up right behind the pilot's head and was deflected up that tube. Why it didn't go on through and kill the kid is a mystery.

A couple of days later Major Tom Lynch flew in and spent a few hours with us. He was the boy's Squadron Commander and at that time was the leading ace in all services. He had 20 confirmed kills, 3 in the P-39. Lynch didn't have much regard for the P-39, he wrote in his journal about a combat action over New Guinea:

> "Could have done better in a truck. It's more maneuverable and will go higher. Could have done damn good with an altitude ship"

Still he was plenty happy to have us escort his fledging flyer back to the home roost and safety. Lynch and Bong flew several missions together and eventually the two of them earned the nick name "The Flying Circus."

Whenever those two flew together it was bad news for the Japanese pilots. Between the two of them they shot down 60 aircraft, with Lynch being promoted to Lieutenant Colonel at the ripe old age of 26. The two were the terrors of the Pacific until Lynch was hit strafing warships over Aitape Harbor and was too low to bail out. He took his P38 Lightening into the water and thus ended a truly great man's story.

I mentioned the event of the Generals going up to view the Ramu river valley. The troops did jump into that place. We heard the sword grass was 20 feet high there but they landed and accomplished their mission. This was the only Allied vertical assault (Para jump) in the Pacific theater, and it was an astounding success.

The first night the men got close to the river where sandy bars had been formed by past floodwaters. The soft sand made an excellent mattress and was good for sleeping. In the morning when roll was checked one man was missing. A man who knew where he had slept was sent to get him. He found where a crocodile had come out of the river and grabbed the soldier dragging him into the river. Tidewater Crocs were known to get very big. Needless to say the Grunts started sleeping a bit more inland and paid as much attention to their rear areas as they did the combat front.

Long before the attack in the Ramu valley there was a pilot named Harris who was assigned to a P-40 squadron at Port Morseby who eventually rose to Squadron Commander. The squadron was getting a great deal of trouble from Jap fighters and the US was beefing up our strength there.

Harris had been written up in one of the periodicals of that time for what I don't remember but we were led to believe the writer was Morris Hecht's brother Ben. Ben Hecht's major claim to success was as a play write and movie scripter. He had some fairly large successes and worked with Alfred Hitchcock and Charles MacArthur.

Ben was very big in magazines and newspapers of that time as a freelance and was a very accurate writer. He had plenty of flash in his writing but being accurate on top was a bonus. We often read the "news" from home and wondered just how dumb we must appear to the general public based off the opinions they would make from some of those lousy stories that had nothing to do with what it was we did but were flashy reads. We were not alone – I heard some Marine ground pounders complaining about the treatment they received by the Post or Look magazines.

Harris took off and was flying on the other side of the Owen Stanley Mountains when a big snake slithered out from under his seat. The guy was justifiably scared and was as we say in the business – combat ineffective. He dropped out of formation and was going home. When the gear is down in a P-40 it leaves the bottom of the ship open and it is probable that the snake climbed up on a wheel strut and up into the cockpit under the pilot's seat. Harris was trying to keep the snake back in the cockpit where it could do no damage, he would pull the stick back and the snake would slide back under the seat, but unfortunately this seemed to only perturb the snake. Harris had no options, he had to keep his feet on the elevator petals and they were directly in front of the snake's intended path.

Finally the snake struck him. He had no way to tell if he was poisoned but began to feel sick. He took his pistol out and started to shoot the snake but was afraid to do so because the main fuel tanks were just below his feet. He made up his mind the snake was going to strike again so he shot the thing. The plane had self-sealing tanks so didn't explode. He was getting sicker by the second and knew he had to land. He put P-40 down alongside the Ramu River in a relatively flat spot that was covered in the tall sword grass. He shut everything down and believes he passed out.

The next morning several men flew out to see if they could find the wreck for that is what they expected to find. He saw them overhead and turned on his radio. Harris wasn't feeling much better but he wasn't deathly sick and felt he could handle the plane. After they talked it over he decided to try and taxi a bit farther in the direction he had landed and then turn around and see if he could get it off along the track he had made while landing.

He pushed the plane a couple of hundred yards down his path, turned around and taxied back to where he had first sat the machine down. He got lined up and he ran the engine up to max and let the brakes off.

The guys watching said they couldn't see the plane in the storm of grass. Being a pilot I can imagine how slow the speed built up but that weary old crate finally dragged itself out of the grass. She must have been hanging on the prop because there could not be a lot of air flowing under that wing. A lesser pilot would not have got that ship out of there but Harris eventually got some altitude and returned the ship to his base. Ground chiefs all over the Pacific now had new inspection checklists which included a step for checking under the seat for any snakes. Harris felt better and did not check in with the docs, he slept off the strike one day and was back in the cockpit the next.

We were very conscious of snakes and the endless bugs in the swamps and jungles while we were there.

Another story was told was about a giant snake. An armed reconnaissance party on our island had been sent out going up the coast trail. They expected to see the enemy at any moment and extreme care was taken. Tactical formations, quiet movement and of course complete silence were the mode of operation that day. Suddenly a man back in the file saw a snake dropping down from the trees above, toward a man in front of him. He opened fire on the snake and yelled out several warning. Once the patrol saw what was happening they were yelling and shooting as well. Tactical security and silence just goes out the window when large snakes are involved and I don't care how well trained you are.

They killed the snake and knowing it was of extreme size they stretched it out on the trail and measured it. It measured 44 feet, bigger than anything in official records of the time.

At the later part of our stay in New Guinea we were extending some of our missions up the North Coast. This day I think we had gone near to Madang which was quite a haul for us and was in "injun" country for a significant part of the flight. Flying in the badlands is always terrifying. Your head is on a "swivel" and you are constantly checking your assigned sector of responsibility. All fighter pilots were issued silk scarfs cause twisting you head in all directions rubbed the neck against the leather collar of the jacket. Even though that jacket is made of the softest leather available, it will cut the back of the neck to the point of running blood if not protected by the silk scarf.

When we flew fighter sweeps or escorts we all had assigned viewing responsibilities. If we were a two ship formation the lead plane's pilot would look forward, right, and bottom. The second plane flying on the lead's left would look left, top, and rear. We constantly swept the skies during flight because an unseen enemy plane coming down was usually very bad news for the unwary one's health record.

Four ship configurations were slightly easier on the neck but pretty much just a hectic. Lead had front and right, his wing left and rear, right lead had right and top, his wing left and bottom. Four ship configurations and anything larger were normal flight strength for us but we routinely used 6 and 8 ship formations which just overlapped the "view" sectors of the first element.

On the way home Collins took us through Kakoda pass so we would come to the drome on the south side. Once above the pass we were just loafing because we didn't have fuel to waste. Without warning of any kind my engine quit. I went over everything I could think of but she wouldn't kick in.

Collins dropped back alongside of me and said: "keep working, I'll tell you when you have to jump." I had checked the tank I was working on and it showed fuel there. Beside that the engine had quit so suddenly I was sure the problem had to be electrical. I was starting to shake. I didn't want to jump and a P-39 with a dead stick has the flight characteristics of a rock – a poorly thrown rock. I didn't have much time. In desperation I shut down all switches and went through the startup procedure all over. Time was running out and I knew it. Collins was giving me a countdown and in under 30 seconds I was going to have to hit the silk. Unfortunately for me – hitting the silk was like advertising you wanted to be shot at by machinegun and rifle fire because we were flying over territory still owned by the enemy.

As suddenly as it quit, my engine started, just like it had never stopped. The mechanics did a detailed inspection of the aircraft but never found anything and it never stopped in midflight again.

My good friend Dan David had been sent to P-40s in New Guinea. As was standard practice in those days he and another replacement were sent up with two old heads in a flight called 'Baptism of Fire.' Captain Bill Harris, the man who had the problem with the snake in the cockpit was the element leader in the flight. Harris is credited with shooting down 16 Japanese planes but never spoke of it. His sole comment was that at least those 16 couldn't shoot him or anyone else down.

They were going along the north side of the Owen Stanley Mountains when somebody looked down and saw two Jap Reccos flying right on the tree tops, obviously to hide from our radar. Harris told the other rookie named Sawyer, to go down and get one. Sawyer slammed the throttle to the firewall and dove like a banshee on the reconnaissance planes and fired everything he had at one of the Reccos. His plane shook from the amount of lead his guns were spitting out and if he hit the mountains you couldn't prove it. Needless to say the Japs continued to fly along. According to Dan – Sawyer missed so badly they didn't realize they were under attack. Harris yelled at him to try again and get it right. They had to hurry or the Japs would run away from the old P-40s. Only their altitude advantage could let them keep up to the Japs.

Sawyer dove again and missed again. He sprayed machinegun bullets all over the pacific and this time alerted the Jap Reccos that there were opposing aircraft in the area. Harris was furious and yelled for Sawyer to get back up. He called David. "You get down there and get one." Dan said he was shaking but dove his P40 building up great speed. Six 50 caliber guns are like a storm but Dan didn't hit anything either. Dan swears he had both planes clearly in his sights and his knuckles were literally bone white squeezing the firing trigger. Harris raved at Dan and he tried again with no better results. Dan missed the rear plane, zoomed past taking fire from the rear gunner and then pulled up hard to take a shot at the lead plane. He fired his guns at the lead to no effect and pulled up right in front of the lead recco who promptly opened up with his two nose mounted guns.

Dan was shanking like a leaf. Harris must have been frothing at the mouth. He ordered Dan to get back up and rejoin the flight. Only the excessive speed that Dan built up in his dive allowed him to do it. Harris rolled into the dive and destroyed both Reccos with the one pass. That was another time Dan laughed 'til I thought he would be sick. Note: Harris' language was less than refined when directed to the rookies and upon landing both were sent back up to practice gunnery drill.

Hatsuyuki (*First Snow*) was the third of twenty-four Fubuki-class destroyers built for the Imperial Japanese Navy following World War I. When introduced into service, these ships were the most powerful destroyers in the world. After significant research on the web this may be the warship George and I sank at the Shortlands.

The Kawasaki Ki-61 *Hien* (flying swallow) was an inline V16 water cooled Japanese fighter used by the Imperial Japanese Army Air Force. We originally thought it to be either a Messerschmitt Bf 109s or an Italian Macchi 205 which led to the code name "Tony". This one was a shock when first encountered because it could dive with our P39s and 40s. National Air and Space Museum (NASM 80-12986), Smithsonian Institution

The Nakajima Ki-43 Hayabusa (Peregrine Falcon) was a single-engine land-based tactical fighter used by the JAAF. The Allied code name was "Oscar". It was significantly slower than the Zero and only mounted 2 12.7mm machineguns in the nose. At the beginning of the war it was a formidable opponent but by 1943 was out of date. We constantly met this bird in action. This sample is a captured Oscar in Chinese markings. Photo by Donald S. Lopez, National Air and Space Museum, Smithsonian Instution (SI 82-4662)

The Kawasaki Ki-45 *Toryu* (Dragon Slayer) was a two-seat, twin-engine fighter code named "Nick". It was fast (336mph), had a high ceiling (32,800 ft) and a range of 1000 miles. In the reconnaissance mode we were VERY lucky to catch one of these. This is the plane involved in the intercept that Jack Little and Ray Bolger made such a comic relief. National Air and Space Museum (NASM 91-14183), Smithsonian Institution

The Nakajima B5N code named Kate was the standard torpedo bomber of the Imperial Japanese Navy (IJN) for much of World War II, however it was routinely used as a land bomber. It had a great range and could carry either 1700 pounds of bombs or a type 91 torpedo. Most of the Kates we met were in bomber configuration. National Air and Space Museum (NASM 83-4546), Smithsonian Institution

The Mitsubishi G4M code named Betty was the main twin-engine, land-based bomber used by the Imperial Japanese Naval Air Service. The G4M had a range of 3,700 miles which was achieved by its structural lightness and an almost total lack of armor plate and self-sealing fuel cells. For defensive armament it had 2 × 20 mm cannon (tail and top turret) and 4 × 7.7 mm machine guns (1 × nose, 2 × waist, 1 × cockpit side) and a bomb load of 2,326 lb. These bombers were constantly attacking our air fields and bases. They often flew at night and were one of the reasons we never got any sleep in World War 2. National Air and Space Museum (NASM 95-1860), Smithsonian Institution

The Mitsubish A6M was the most respected enemy aircraft. The Zero - named for the imperal year 2600 (1940 in the Gregorian calendar) singlehandedly changed American fighter thought. In Japan it was referred to as bothRei-sen and Zero-sen but the Japanese pilots most commonly called it Zero-sen. With a speed of 331 mph it was both fast and maneuverable. Two 7.7 mm machine guns and two 20mm cannon in the wings made this plane a formidable weapon, which unfortunately was placed in the best pilots' hands. With a range of 1900 miles it was able to hit us from almost anywhere. It was almost suicide to dogfight one of these birds with a P40 or P39 and plenty of P38s found their doom as well. This was the best the Japanese had and they had plenty of them. The weakness of no self-sealing fuel tanks and little personal armor were compensated for by greater advantages in dog fighting. National Air and Space Museum (NASM 91-13132), Smithsonian Institution.

WOODLARK

23 July 1943 - 19 Aug 1943

We were told that we would be sent forward again. This time to a tiny island called Woodlark in the Trobriand group. It was about a hundred fifty miles north of Milne Bay. Woodlark fell to the US troops in Operation Chronicle and was attacked by the 112 Cavalry Regiment which could well be the regiment of horse I saw in the 41 maneuvers. The Texan 112 Cavalry was federalized in 1940 and was shipped over to New Caledonia in 1942 where it was thought the horse Cavalry could provide rapid response security.

Unfortunately the torrential Pacific rains and the mud that followed damaged the horses' hooves and the horses were sent to the Burma Theater to assist the Chinese. The 112 made an unopposed landing at Woodlark as dismounted Cavalry and set up security on June 30th. The 60th US Naval Construction Battalion followed immediately after. The CBs built a single 3,000 feet x 150 feet coral surfaced runway and we moved in before construction was complete. The runway was expanded to 6,500 feet x 225 feet with a parallel runway of 6,000 feet x 60 feet and 110 hardstands by the time we left. It was to be a major launch point for the war. I have mixed feelings about this base.

At first Woodlark was a wonderful dead time. I never figured why we were there. There wasn't anybody there to shoot at us. The Japs would send over six ship bomber flights at night once in a while just to remind us they were the neighborhood but that was just nuisance – not so much from the bombers flying about but all the racket and commotion caused by the anti-aircraft cannons. The anti-aircraft guys would burn about a million dollars worth of ammunition every time a bomber formation came over but never hit anything to my knowledge.

Collins was sent up there to inspect and see if the strip was ready. When he returned he couldn't get his gear down and had to belly land. He set it down on the grass between the steel planking of the runway and the ditch. He did a perfect job. He killed the engine before the prop touched so the engine wasn't damaged. The bird was back on the line in a week. He was the best natural pilot I ever saw and was one heck of a leader.

The new strip on Woodlark was built by the Seabees. They must have been told how long the runway had to be so they went across the beach into the jungle and cut out the exact measurement they were given. The jungle was about a hundred feet high so we were delayed until an approach could be cut. The strip was made of pulverized ground coral which when packed with the steamrollers they had made it as hard as concrete. The Seabees made that strip the hardest and smoothest I ever saw anywhere before or since. The strip was so well built that after the war those strips became the civilian air ports for all the islands. I have heard that some of the original strips are still being used to this day.

They were posted to the island so they built their area just off the runway on the jungle side. The runway was right against the ocean. The pilots' tents were out in the jungle safely away from any targets. The layout for that base was perfect and it was designed (in my mind at least) with safety first.

A retread General was the commander of the Cavalry Regiment at Woodlark. He had been a cavalry officer during his active duty days and had no use for airplanes or the people who worked with them and he let that be well known. Now one would think that by 1943 the value of the airplane had been clearly established but apparently not so. Of course there are still people who think the earth is flat.

That General violated not only the SOP for airfields and aircraft; he violated common sense and simply safety when dealing with high performance technical wonders that had a heavy mechanical component. The General didn't like the lay out of the base, couldn't understand tactical disbursement, and basically wanted all the pilots and ground crew in parade uniform every day. I think he thought us to be some wild bunch that just needed some old fashioned discipline to square them away.

Hecht received some strange order on reporting how much toilet paper our squadron was using (something like that). He took it in the good natured way of a junior command being generally harassed by the senior command so the junior command would be properly put in its place. He had a good laugh as did the rest of the squadron and the following day a Cavalry Lieutenant was knocking on Hecht's door asking for the report. Slowly it dawned on the good Major that the Cavalry command was sincere in its ludicrous request and he blew his top. Here he was trying to get a squadron and all its operational and logistical support organized and some fool wanted to know how much toilet paper was used.

Not one time did the General get in a cockpit and go up to fight, he never ran three to six missions a day and he definitely never had to "go" in a coke bottle over 200 miles of water. He tried to tell us how the aircraft would be managed and handled and wanted to line up the fighters in neat straight line rows as if we never learned anything from the attack on Pearl Harbor.

Major Hecht finally told the General that he was the senior flying officer present and would make all decisions regarding airplanes, pilots and logistical support needed to keep the planes in operational condition. The advantage of being in general support vice attached to the Cavalry was that our squadron had its own reporting chain of command and they were further up the totem pole than the commander from the Cav.

Don't know what happened from there but evidently someone higher up thought close air support was more valuable than planes and pilots being cleaned and shined and we never had any further issue. We always kept our planes disbursed and in revetments, even if they didn't look ready for parade, and I don't think we reported toilet paper usage for the rest of the war.

I was sent off to Guadalcanal to pick up the mail and was tooling around the base waiting for the mail to be sorted. I had the duty that afternoon so I was not in a particular hurry to get back. I saw a brand new C-47 Skytrain as we now called the DC3s sitting on the strip. Turns out that was the transport for a USO show with Ray Bolger and singer song writer Little Jack Little. They had recently completed a couple of shows for the troops at Guadalcanal and were going to New Guinea but the schedule was messed up and they had that evening free. Using my best command initiative I invited them to do a show at Woodlark and they agreed. I flew escort to the C-47 and we landed at the strip. I brought the two huge acts to meet the CO and then got called into the OPS hut, I had the duty so I was supposed to be in the hut.

It wasn't long before the operator on duty said he had a bogy. We talked a bit with the several people were in the symposium. I asked the operator if he could tell how high the target was and he said the bogy was about a hundred miles out but he could only tell us he was very high.

I said that tells me he is probably a Recco. That makes sense because this is a new installation the Japs would want to have a look at us. I recommended they order two fighters on the ready strip to launch. They did that. They got Ops on the phone and based on our discussion told the ready flight if the bogy started in and remains high we would have to launch two additional fighters. If the fighters had to go to max altitude they would use a great deal of fuel, particularly when running at 'Buster' meaning maximum power.

A trick reccos used was to make believe they were making the pass, but then suddenly turn away and disappear off our radar screens and the interceptors that were launched using full power and thus full gas would run short of fuel. The standing patrol was on the way down when their replacements reached twenty thousand and a third two were rolling out to the ready strip. It took 6 minutes to get a plane to altitude for a fight so some decisions had to be made on less than perfect information. Radar said the recco had straightened out and was coming in very fast. I told the operator I believed he would come in this time and launched the ready fighters.

When we had the fighters climbing up we had them over the opposite side of the island because we didn't want the Jap to see them. The recco was much too fast for us. If he saw us he'd leave us in his dust.

The radar people had plotted the problem and now ordered the vector. The pilots were informed where and how high the bandit was. In just a couple of minutes one of the pilots called "Tally Ho" just like an English Fox hunter. The pilot had the altitude advantage he needed and now the Jap was as good as dead, which he was in two minutes more.

The Jap plane was a new one to us. It was called was an Irving, a twin engine with excellent performance at altitude. Originally designed as a two seat fighter for bomber escort, the plane was found to be unsuitable for that role and was converted to two versions, a night fighter and a recon bird. The recon version had a top speed of 330 and very well could get away from us especially at altitude where our ships pretty much just sat in the air. The General had a radio in his bunker and the entertainers had listened to all the jargon that went on between the radar and the pilots.

That evening was the usual party so the entertainers could put on their program. It was held in the Ops Quonset hut; the General didn't come but his guests were there to do their job. They had performed in several places around the island during the day.

Ray Bolger had more fun than anybody else. He was a happy man and communicated it to others. Little Jack Little had an accordion. Being a piano player he couldn't bring that. He never used his left hand for playing except to hold the instrument. When asked about that he said: "I don't have any idea what all that stuff is for."

During the evening they got to horsing around with the pilots who had made the kill and would try to imitate the conversations. Since they didn't have even a glimmer of what the words meant it took on a very funny connotation to us and many of our drunks almost collapsed laughing.

Bolger sat in a chair and had a broom stick for a control stick. He rolled his aircraft and did loops, hammer heads, and Immelmanns, all with extended commentary and exaggerated body activity – there has never been anything so funny before or since, we rolled with laughter.

Jack Little was the Radar Operator. For about ten minutes they had everyone in stitches. I think their performance was better than the planned performances. Jack sang. We broke in on him all the time. Bolger danced. I think Bolger could see I was older than the rest and not drunk. He spoke to me for an extended time and I think he was sincerely interested in what we were doing there.

The next day the courier came in. The two guys were supposed to be ready but there were hundreds of men around clamoring for Ray to dance. Some of the men went in our Ops shack and hauled out a big table we had built and Ray danced on that.

Soon the pilots of the gooney bird were getting the men in the plane. They were just shutting the door when Ray reached out and took my hand. He said "if ever you are any place where I am working come back and visit with me." I have always thought he meant it but never took him up on his offer. He passed away in 1987 and was the last living member of the 1939 Wizard of Oz movie.

MacArthur had made a treaty with the king of the Trobriands. There were three groups of islands in his realm and all were close together. The most important item of the agreement was that the King would bring all the women to the center island and no white man would be allowed to go there. That was Gowa, a little round island for which the king received considerable compensation for moving all his wives to that island. He was offered a large palace constructed by the SeaBees and a fairly substantial subsistence to maintain two palaces.

MacArthur informed his commanders that agreement would be observed and the King's ladies were off limits. One day some of our men on patrol saw an outrigger out at sea and went down to look it over. One of the guys went too close and his prop blast turned the canoe over. It was the king and beside his paddlers he had a couple of his wives with him. That report came down through channels and our General was going to make an example of someone.

The General suspended all flying and had all pilots fall out and come to attention. "I want to know who blew the canoe over." Of course this question had been asked in our own briefing and nobody admitted to it. They didn't know. The guy that did it (If indeed it was our squadron) might not have known he was responsible because it had been established that the flight had gone by at high speed and in loose formation. Unless the leader had looked back nobody else would.

The General ordered that everybody would stand there, at attention until the offender stepped forward and then he promptly left. Hecht ignored that order and sent the report back stating the leader of the flight had received a verbal reprimand.

The General wasn't through with us yet. He came over and had us fall in. He didn't mention the outrigger incident or that we had been dismissed. He said something to the effect that he had a job and needed men with high qualifications. He walked up and down the formation a couple of times and stopped in front of me and smiled. He said: "Lieutenant the job I want done has the possibility of considerable danger to it. Will you accept the job?"

I said "Sir you do me honor to even consider me."

The second man was a good friend of mine named Pappy Davis. I'm quite sure he just stepped forward. The General handed a written order to Hecht and spun around and left.

The order said there was reason to think there were Jap coast watchers on the opposite side of the island. The other pilot Pappy and I were to see if we could find them. This was to be a ground reconnaissance and why pilots were performing this task was beyond understanding. Hecht was prepared to go battle the General again over the silly orders but Pappy and I said we could use a good walk and the mechanics could pull the 100 hour checks on our birds. At this point the Japs were not contesting our landing at Woodlark yet, so Hecht let it go and Pappy and I went off for our adventure. We drew some rifles and rounds of ammunition. We got a couple of C-Rations, two canteens and that was about it. I did take a blanket and my mosquito bar because the "mission" was on the far end of the island and we would be sleeping under the stars that night. It was a totally bogus op, any Japs on the island would have been discovered by the natives and they had little liking for the Japs.

I don't know who arranged it but there was an Army Higgins boat ready for us. A Sergeant was the operator of that thing. We boarded and exchanged pleasantries but he was a quiet man. He never asked where we were going and we didn't think to ask if he knew where we were going. We went around the end of the island and down the opposite side landing at a fishing village. The soldier must have known it was there because he went right to it, dropped us off, and backed right out and left. And that is how the Army Air Force's assault invasion of Woodlark landing started.

The small village had something like ten shacks and where we made our landing there were maybe eight or ten children playing in the surf and sand. Of course they ganged around us happy to see strangers and we "battled" our way through them by handing out candy bars. If we had planned any stealth to this operation it was lost amongst the screaming and laughing of the kids.

We fooled with them for a bit until I saw a monstrous tree growing out over the water. It was leaning so far over I could almost walk up it. I got out quite a ways and realized I could see the bottom, which was probably 15 feet deep at that spot and was a flat rock shelf.

As I looked down I could see many fish and some were quite large. I got the idea to shoot in the water, close to one and see if I could stun it. Each time one would come close to the surface I would do that. The kids were watching and when a fish surfaced they all raced for it. I did this maybe four or five times and each fish was retrieved and handed over to the sub chief of the island.

I realize this is not exactly a "tactical" maneuver but when we were in the Higgins boat the Sergeant clearly was astounded that we would go hunting mythical Japs – any Jap on the island would have long ago been dispatched by the natives as they had no used for them. That pretty much set the tone for the rest of the mission. We were being sent out here to "punish" us and we were going to take full advantage of the situation.

I noticed one of the kids retrieving that night's dinner was a female. She was as wild in the water as the boys and swam as good as the fish. The native people were brown skin with what struck me as a tinged of yellow. Their hair was a great bush that was carefully fixed into a smooth orb. Their hair was brown tending to orange and all were exactly the same. They were a very handsome people but the girl was different. Her hair was black as jet and while she was brown it was from the sun.

Two other features about her were distinctive. Her teeth were white where all the adults' were black. Adults, I learned, chewed Betel Nut which blackened their teeth. The girl was half cast and I learned that she could never marry in the tribe. She could never progress beyond the status of a servant. This little girl had no status in the tribe so she was here with a couple of very old women who were there to serve the sub Chief in charge.

The Chief invited us to supper that evening and told us he was pleased with the gift of the fish. He spoke Pidgin English and during the meal the little girl went in and out several times. As she went by I was talking to him and he noticed I was glancing at her. He said: "you want?" I shook my head no. He must have realized what I had thought and quickly said "No, No. You take. You keep. You give $20.00."

All he wanted was to get rid of her. The girl would be treated about like a pet dog. Her father was a Portuguese gold miner who had simply left the island and abandoned her and I never found out what happened to her mother. She was a spectacularly beautiful girl. Her teeth were perfect and gleaming white. Hair was black and hung down her back in contrast to all the natives. Her skin was tan rather than brown, her eyes were blue. Her figure was just starting to develop and she was slender as a willow wand. I have wondered what MacArthur would have said if he heard I was raising a girl child in my tent.

I later spoke to a lady in the Red Cross from Auckland and asked if something could be done to get the child out of there. She knew of a priest who did something along that line and she promised to speak to him. That was the girl's only chance.

After dinner, the old Chief showed us some ebony he wanted to sell. I have to believe that was where his money came from. I finally settled on a cube of Ebony about 8 inches square. It was polished to a "you can see yourself" shine and was just beautiful. I noticed I could not detect any grain in the wood. I paid him twenty dollars for it. I think Pappy bought some sort of carved figure.

In talking to the men we learned that there were no Japs on the island. If there were they would have been captured and I felt, from the talk, they would never see their homeland again. Pappy and I talked and decided we would leave in the morning. Since no arrangement had been made we figured to walk. The natives showed us a trail going out in the jungle.

As we walked we saw several pineapple farms. They were too heavy to carry so we didn't buy any however many of the farmers offered a sample of their wares, which Pappy and I did avail ourselves. They were sweet and juicy; if they had been but chilled it would have been the definition of paradise. Late in the afternoon we came out in the clear and saw we were close to the radar station that was sitting on the only hill on the island. The hill was about 300 feet high and the station was built on an abandoned gold mine. The Germans had used the hill in WWI for a radio station and the famed German raider, SMS Emden, had stopped there as well.

We struggled up the hill and somebody saw us and alerted the officer in charge. A Navy Lieutenant JG invited us into his quarters which was a wooden shack. He had a dilapidated kerosene operated refrigerator. He reached in there and drew out a big pineapple. He cut each of us a generous slice of the vine ripened fruit. It was the sweetest, juiciest, ice cold most pleasing thing I have ever eaten.

The JG said: 'sorry gentlemen only one 'cause this is all I got left.' One of the farmers made a weekly supply run to the station and they loaded up on the fantastic food. We spent some time going through the station and met several of the guys we talked to over the radio during the missions. Finally it was getting close to dark when the JG said; "we better get down to the dock. Your ride is coming in now."

When the "naval war ship" came alongside it could only be described as a party boat. She was about 40 feet long, white with mahogany decks and rails, shiny brass railing and a small dance hall on the stern. We went aboard and paid respects to the flag and were then introduced to the officer standing behind us.

He was an ancient Commander who had been recalled to service years after his retirement. His ship was on loan to the navy for the duration and had not been modified, no combat paint job or weapons mounted. Our Naval Commander turned out to be a congenial man who wanted to sit and tell stories.

First he ordered a report on our mission. Then he said we were going to have supper on the after deck. That turned out to be charcoal grilled steak. I would have been willing to do the mission over if I could get another one of those. I thought the Navy must not eat many

C-Rations. He told us about his combat duty in WWI and apparently the drafted party boat had a well-stocked liquor cabinet that came with the boat. We socialized while the boat was underway and it wasn't long after that we were put alongside a little narrow dock and we bid him goodbye.

We reported our findings to Hecht and never heard anything further. Pappy and I both volunteered to do any further reconnaissance missions the General might have in mind. The entire evolution was a joke, it was an attempt to punish some of the flyboys by making them walk through the big scary jungle on the island. It was one of the most pleasant times I had during the war.

A new arrival was assigned as my wingman and he was a dandy young man named George Dumas. We got on as the say in the movies rather famously and he was a quick study. Me being the old head and having actually lived long enough to know better I had his full attention when we discussed tactics or flying topics and tips. Later, he and I were sent on an Able, Charlie search. That is a simple search around the coastline. Our part was the Northeast quarter of the coast. We didn't see anything until I made a circle over Monatu Point.

On these searches we always carried a 500 pound general purpose bomb in case something worth attacking was discovered. Even in our N models our bases were close enough to the action that we didn't need the center line drop tanks. In some cases too close as standard Jap light artillery would often take pot shots at us.

As we searched the coastline below us I drifted toward Monatu Point and by remotest chance saw a ship through a slit in the foliage. I couldn't believe my eyes. This was a big ship. Probably 200 feet long which puts it in the heavy destroyer or light cruiser class. How the Japs had worked it into that swamp I can't even guess. But she was there.

I hadn't noticed before but my gun sight was out. I told George I would make a hip shot with my 500 pounder but I wanted him to sight below the stack and try to get it in the water beside the hull. The concussion of a 500 pound bomb would cave in the side of the ship and cause most likely fatal damage if the bomb could be placed close enough.

I put my 500 pound general purpose bomb in the side of the ship on line with the rear stack. It was a good hit and the ship rocked with the explosion. George came around and I saw he had lost the target. I called him on the radio trying to direct him by voice but he could not pick up the outline of the ship. I had a clear view of the target so I told him to follow me and he could pick it up again that way.

He followed me in and when he picked up the target he called me off so he could make a clear bomb run. I circled back and saw his weapon arc down and hit the water about ten yards short of the ship's side. A perfect hit. I was tickled so much I yelled. The explosion sent an eruption of water 250 feet in the air and caved in the side of the ship. He must have taken the bottom out of that ship 20 feet square and we could see it settling as we pulled out.

I told George "I'll bet if they sleep in there tonight it will be wet." I have thought about that several times. I imagine the Japs were getting ready to move it and had taken the camouflage off it in preparation for the move. It must have been some kind of desperate mission because the Jap Navy didn't move much in the South Pacific Seas during the daylight. That would be the only way we could see it.

Doing some research for this piece I tried to see if I could identify the ship with the time and the location of the action and determine if our ship was listed in the Japanese ship directory. I am not positive but the Japanese Destroyer Hatsuyuki seems to fit all the characteristics of the attack – Wikipedia says: "On 17 July 1943, while docked at Shortlands unloading passengers at position, 6° 50' S and 155° 47'E Hatsuyuki was attacked in an air strike by USAAF aircraft. A bomb exploded the after magazine, sinking her in shallow water, with 120 dead (including 38 passengers) and 36 wounded."

If this is the ship she was a main battle component for the INJ having assisted in sinking two Allied Cruisers, HMAS Perth and USN Houston, as well as 3 US destroyers and had provided numerous landing supports. Destroyer number 30 had 6 127mm cannon, 22 25mm anti-aircraft cannon, 9 torpedo tubes and 36 depth charges. It could move at 38 knots with a range of 5000 nautical miles. That ship was too dangerous to be left floating.

We once again had bitter fighting on the northern Solomons as the US Marines and the Army's 37th Division were preparing to attack the

Island of Bougainville which history has shown began on November 1, 1943. We had a spilt command again – part of the squadron was in Woodlark and part was shipped back to Guadalcanal in September, and we flew out of any base in-between. It was truly a total free for all and the CO had a tough time tracking just where all his pilots were. From mid-August through the first part of September we flew mainly out of Woodlark and supported both the Army and Marines whenever we were called. Again it was one of those 4-7 missions a day and we had been going for two full weeks.

The Japs weren't caught sleeping and were giving us as good as they got. We'd fly and fight all day and at night the Japs would bomb or shell the field. When the field was attacked the sirens would blare and everyone would have to jump out of their cots and race for the bomb shelters. As soon as the all clear was sounded we'd run back to our cots and the rotten Japs would send over another plane or shoot some more artillery at us. Sleep became a vague memory and I had to yell into my microphones to wake more than one exhausted pilot that had fallen asleep in the air.

On the ground once we taxied to the prep areas for refueling and rearming the pilots often slept in the cockpit or on the ground right next to the field. I am not saying it wasn't tough on the ground crews, but when the planes were in the air they could catch a cat nap, granted they worked all night long getting our birds in commission so everyone on the island needed more sleep.

I was no exception, I was exhausted and flight leads had to show up early for briefings and then take the briefing to their flight so everyone knew what we were supposed to be doing. One squadron could and routinely did have multiple roles at the same time, element of 2 for patrolling, element of 4 for search and destroy to the north, element of 2 for recon to the south east, one for parts run to the depot, two on ready strip, and one in the maintenance hangar for annual services. At this time we had 27 fighters and 23 pilots and we were all in the air all the time. After four missions two with deep strikes I finally told my crew I was going to sleep in my rack tonight and if the bombs dropped or the island got shelled too bad so sad I was not leaving my rack period.

I dove into the rack and joined the zombies – I was gone to this world. I was sleeping soundly and heard the Jap bomber before the sirens started to scream, but muffled my ears with my pillow and turned over. I was snoring hard when Hecht grabbed my shirt and screaming at me told me to get my shoes and get in the bunker.

I had never seen Hecht lose it like that but with no one sleeping I guess I could forgive him. Everyone was on a short string and I was supposed to be in the bunker. I threw on my shoes, didn't tie them and raced off to the bunker. I flew in and stumbled on the coral stairs leading to the shelter and sliced up my knee. I wailed in pain and everyone in the bunker looked at me like I was some kind of idiot. Collins yelled at me demanding to know why I was so late to the bunker and I said I was going to sleep in until Hecht dragged me out of the rack.

Despite the racket of the bombs, somehow everyone in the bunker heard what I had said and looked at me like I had lost my mind.

"What did you say Case?" said Collins looking me straight in the face.

"I was going to sleep in but Major Hecht dragged me out of the rack and made me come in the shelter." I replied wondering what was going on as I rubbed my skinned knees.

"Major Hecht?" said Collins putting his hand on my head to see if I had a fever and looking at me real serious.

"Yea Captain Major Hecht, he grabbed me out of the rack and told me to get in the bunker - what is wrong?" I asked completely confounded.

"Hecht's plane fell apart last week. He's not with us Bob." said Collins as if talking to a small child.

It finally dawned on me that Hecht, being the true leader that he was and taking his share of the lousy duty, had scrambled from the ready takeoff after a recon bird and his plane had literally fallen apart in the sky. There was no reason for it, it was well maintained and Hecht was meticulous in attention to detail on preflight. He was killed August 18, 1943 and the world was not a better place for it.

I was stunned because to this very day I know Hecht woke me up and forced me out of my rack. Some psychoanalyst may make up some feeble reason as to why I think Hecht pulled me out of the rack but if

I was a cursing man I'd let loose on him. I don't think Hecht pulled me out of the rack; I know he pulled me out of the rack and I don't care if he did die the week before. It is one of the unexplained from the battle front.

When the all clear was sounded I headed back to the squad bay where we slept and one of the bombs had blown up one of our Quonset huts. One of the main support spars had been launched in the air and was projecting out of the pallet we used for a floor directly under my bed. Had I not left my rack, that spar would have gone right through me and I would not be writing this story, or it would be significantly shorter.

Morris Hecht was killed August 18 1943 and Collins became the permanent CO August 19th. Collins had been CO several times before when Hecht had been on R&R or called back to the rear to handle some admin stuff so the transition was easy. When the squadron was split, Collins was always assigned to lead one of the sections.

Before I became a flight lead Collins and I had been pretty good friends, when I became a flight lead Collins and I were best friends despite his rank of Captain. His promotion to CO didn't change much in the way the squadron operated. Yes we missed Hecht and it would have been nice not to lose him but we did and the mission remained. Collins was the same kind of leader, one of the follow me men and you never needed to try and find where he was – he was always at the front. Some people march to the sound of battle, Collins ran to it.

I think Collins was the best pilot I have ever met and I met some Air Force heavyweights, Welch, Bong, Lynch, Lanphier the list is lengthily, but no one could handle any aircraft the way Collins could. He tried to pass on all the info he could to all the pilots, not only the fledging junior birdmen but the old heads who had been around for forever. This on occasion caused some problems.

I mentioned I got to be a pallbearer five times at Woodlark, one of them was a kid I had taken under my wing who was trying to recover from a less than stellar performance at New Caledonia. This kid had lost a P-38 Lightening and had been transferred to us when we first got to New Caledonia. I did some flight indoctrination with him and the P-39 and he appeared to be picking up the quirks of the plane.

It was a rainy day and visibility was poor but passable. Collins and my "student" had taken off earlier in the morning for a patrol of the bay and the second shift patrol planes had a mechanical issue so they were late getting off for relief. Collins and the kid were low on fuel so they pretty much were committed to landing at the Woodlark strip despite the weather. Collins rolled in and touched down as if it was a concrete pad and perfect weather conditions. The kid tried to follow him in but he wasn't good enough. He stalled the P-39 and it killed him. He should not have been in fighters.

We lost another pilot while we were rat racing after a mission. Collins had us in trail and doing simple acrobatics. We busted through a little cumulus cloud and the guy was missing when we came out. He had been right behind me. The natives showed us where to find the remains. This man was one of the older pilots and nothing was new or difficult to him. It was never explained.

I have seen several Hollywood war movies where the CO yells at the rookie pilot for doing a loop or a barrel roll after a battle and the comment "what if your plane had been damaged? Those crazy stunts could make you crash!" or some other garbage line. I never saw a CO who chewed out a pilot for acrobatics ever. In every squadron I was in and supported we were encouraged to stunt the aircraft and we had regular competitions as well. Rat Racing was the most common form of recreation in the war and all it did was make us better pilots.

After 90 some missions I got another R&R this time to New Zeeland and after the normal check in had a great time exploring the cities and the country side. New Zeeland is a land of stunning beauty.

I was checking out to go back to Woodlark and somebody told us Dan David was in the hospital at Moresby. Our ride was headed over to Moresby where I could catch a connecting flight back to Woodlark. There was another man from my squadron on that plane and somebody told me that guy was acting strange. He wasn't supposed to be there. I got a seat next to him and found he didn't know where he was going. Later in the flight I realized it wasn't anything temporary, the man had lost it completely.

At Moresby I got him to go with me when I told him Dan was in the hospital and I wanted to see him. We stopped by a doctor's office and the doctor only talked to the guy for a moment and knew what was wrong. He called for some people and they took the man away. They left him sitting in some waiting room alone. A female nurse walked in and he attacked her and almost killed her before help arrived. We had that happen again later with another pilot. He did exactly the same thing as if working from a script

This guy's name was Jeane. When I rotated back to the States I saw him once more walking across the ramp at Pinellas. He was carrying a parachute going to a plane. We talked a bit and he said he was going back again to see if he could do it right this time.

I had flown an intercept with him one time and he was the wildest craziest man I ever flew with. We took off and before the plane was ready to lift off he racked back forcing the engine to lift the plane so he could pull his landing gear in and get more speed. I was never more frightened in that war. He left contrails a foot wide and was completely reckless in the air, now he was a quiet man and flew very conservatively. I never heard anything of him again.

The Army had just declared this part of New Guinea to be a rear area. That meant female personnel could be assigned there, hence the female nurse. I went to the hospital and saw Dan. He was a mess and I could not understand why he was still alive. If he had unbroken bones, I couldn't guess where.

There were ropes and harnesses all over him; every part of his body that could move was in a cast. He was conscious and he was glad to see me. He was rational and told me what happened to him.

His squadron was on a mission up the coast and his bird (P-40) got hit hard. He left the formation to go home but he was spewing oil out of the engine and within a few minutes the engine quit.

We had all been told never to try to belly land in the jungle, if there was an option of belly landing do it in the sea and swim to shore. Dan had looked down and saw a wash that looked like diamonds along the side of a clear running stream. It looked good so he decided to violate the belly landing rule and set down in that nice soft sand. He didn't want to jump with the parachute, but then nobody else did either.

He made a good approach and was rounding out for the touchdown when he saw the riverbed was eroded in great big waves, just like ocean waves. It was dry, baked clay about as hard as a rock. According to Dan it was exactly noon with the sun directly above so the shadows of the dunes were nonexistent. With a dead engine and gliding an 8000 lb plane he had no option; he had to continue what he started. The airplane hit and was ripped to pieces. He lost his wings right off the bat as they were ripped off by huge boulders along his path which also went unobserved. The plane's tail broke off and his plane skidded sideways where another boulder separated his engine from his cockpit. His cockpit rolled and shattered his canopy and when everything stopped there was nothing but the cockpit left with Dan sitting in it. He was unconscious.

He regained consciousness. He doesn't know when but he was reaching around with the one arm he could move. He was trying to find his Flight Log. He doesn't know why but thinks he wanted to report that one of the gages on his machine no longer functioned properly. He looked around as much as he could and decided to get out onto the stub of the left wing so he could stretch out. Of course he couldn't move at all and promptly passed out again.

He awakened and thought his plane would be on fire and he had to get out. He wanted to pull off his quick release and then promptly passed out again. He didn't wake until the next morning, he thinks. Sometime later he woke again and thought he had to get out of the plane but couldn't get the quick release to actually release. After passing out again he awoke and saw some natives around him, one was trying to unfasten his harness. These guys had bones in their noses and ears and lips. They also had gruesome masks painted on their faces. We all had been told there were still cannibals in the deep jungles and these folks were the perfect example of such.

Dan reached for his gun intending to shoot them but couldn't make it and he fainted again. When he woke again he was on a litter being carried by the same natives, probably to the stew pot, and he tried to go for his gun again, though the natives had taken it. He passed out again. The natives took him to an Aussie coast watcher who had organized the crew to scout for him. The Aussie gave him primitive first aid and bandaged as many of the holes as he could. He forced Dan to drink some water and called in the pilot's condition in his next report.

The Aussie command sent the Navy to make the rescue. From the description it was either a corvette or a destroyer escort. The Captain of the ship came up the river crashing through trees and sunken logs. I have no idea how that boat made it up the river but Dan was there in the hospital so it had to be true. There was no place to turn the ship around so once they had retrieved Dan they backed down the river to the sea.

Dan said they were trying to fix him enough to get him back to the States where he could heal. That would be a while I was sure.

I started to leave but Dan said 'wait a minute. I want to tell you about Sawyer.' I turned back and sat down. I remember saying, "What has that guy done now?"

Dan was laughing if you could call it that. He must have been in pain but he couldn't control it. When he started laughing he convulsed in pain but he couldn't stop laughing and I thought he was going to break something again. Tears started to roll down his face and I told him to take it easy

He started off with "you probably know we were exchanging aircraft. The way we did it was we would take one down to the depot and then the pilot would exchange the war weary bird for a brand new or rebuild bird and bring that one back to the base."

"The Squadron Commander saw Sawyer and said for him to take his ship down for exchange and that he could visit me for a command visitation at the same time."

Sawyer landed at the depot and pulled into the parking area. With a P-40 the pilot would unbuckle and step out on the wing. Sawyer did that and reached in and got the after-flight form. It only took seconds to fill that out and toss it back in the seat. The pilot would spin around and step off on to the wheel and bounce on to the ground.

Well Sawyer did that or started to do that and his leg was extended toward the wheel when he saw a Red Cross girl standing there with coffee and doughnuts. The Army had declared the area a secure zone and the Red Cross thought it a good idea to meet the pilots as they returned from a mission with coffee and doughnuts, much the way the Brits were doing in Europe. Sawyer was so startled to see a beautiful woman standing there he missed the wheel and landed flat on his face. The fall broke his arm and they put him in the bed next to Dan.

I've laughed at that story many times but couldn't laugh as hard as Dan when he told it. He was laughing and couldn't stop. He was in awful pain but for his life couldn't stop.

Dan shot down two Japanese planes before being hit and evacuated back to the States. He was awarded the Distinguished Flying Cross with Oak Leaves, several Air Medals and the Purple Heart. When he rotated back he started his comedy show with Dick Martin using his stage name Dan Rowan and married the 1945 Miss America runner up Phyllis Mathis. He had a successful career as a comedy duo and when the show "Laugh In" went on TV it was the number one show for years.

Pappy Davis caught up with me and we flew back to Milne Bay and found it was almost deserted. The people who ran the tower were still there and they said the courier was still running. Davis and I hopped a courier and went to Woodlark. That was worse than Milne Bay. The tower people were still working but the base was nearly deserted. They told us an LSI (Landing Ship Infantry) had pulled in to the beach and loaded the entire squadron's equipment and personal gear on the LSI while the ground crew was loaded to mike boats (LCM). All the aircraft had been flown out by the pilots.

The personnel who manned the tower were Aussies. Their Commander was on the island to the west of us. They said they would get in touch with him and tell him we were marooned.

We also heard that the LCI the squadron had put all its equipment in was attacked and sunk and all our stuff was lost. My ebony souvenir and all my personal gear went down with the ship. Pappy's as well. After I thought about it for a while I got to thinking that I hoped all the people were able to get out of the ship and that my gear could be replaced, but it was still a tragic loss as I could never replace that piece of wood.

Our squadron people had traveled by mike boat and landed safely at Guadalcanal. Don't know why the squadron support folks were separated from the gear but it was a good thing. In some ways it was a great thing in that the maintenance section had to be fully outfitted and got not only all the tools and supplies they were supposed to have – most of it was brand new and in full working order.

Two days later a British Beaufighter came in and the pilot told us he was supposed to take us back to Guadalcanal. He said we can make it if we leave now, so we climbed into the fuselage and tried to get comfortable. Right at that time I started to feel bad. This airplane was a gun ship; the entire floor of the fuselage was covered with .30 Cal machine guns, and four 20mm cannon. The observer seat had been removed so we could fit inside so the only seats were some flimsy blankets thrown over the guns. We sat on the guns and I prayed real hard, "Lord please don't let him fire those guns." Any action involving gunfire would tear up our lower extremities.

We were well on our way when the pilot asked me what the entry procedure at the Canal was. I told him I didn't know they had one and he gave me a very sour look as if he was truly dealing with rank amateurs and this was a perfect example of how America was ruining the war. I truly believe he was mad he didn't get to throw a gauntlet at the Japanese before flying in at them. We finally got down and I got off those guns with sore spots all over my posterior. Pappy and I vowed not to do that one again.

Lightning

This is the one we all wanted to fly. It was fast (445MPH with combat boost), powerful, and could get to altitude (44,000 ft). With a range of 1,300 miles it could roam the South Pacific at will and with four .50 cal machineguns and a 20mm cannon it had enough fire power to bring down the toughest competition. All the big names in the Pacific ended up with this bird, Bong, McGuire, Welch, and Lamphier to name a few. The conversion of the 67th was delayed just long enough for them to not be fitted with the Lightening at all – they converted to P47. National Air and Space Museum, (NASM 75-15985) Smithsonian Institution.

This is the bird made famous by General Clair Chennault and the Flying Tigers. Though most of us felt the P-40 was a better plane overall than the P-39, it was uncomfortable to fly and had a tendency yaw. Gun power was up to six .50 cal wing mounted machineguns. It wasn't as fast as the 39 and the range was almost the same, it did of course have our missing turbocharger and could get to 29,000 feet. Dan David – later Dan Rowan got two kills in this bird before being shot down over New Guinea. National Air and Space Museum, Smithsonian Institution (SI 76-3248-4).

This is the bottom line – the P39 with .30 and .50 caliber machineguns, a 37mm cannon, and a 500 pound bomb load was the work horse for the ground support role. We flew more missions than any other squadron in theater.

Collins at Woodlark before he met his girl in Australia. He was the best pilot in the Pacific theater bar none.

After complaining enough the General delivered on his promise and let us have an "additional" plane on the roster. We would have contests and drawings to see who got to fly the P40 shown above. I won this round and got to get my picture taken with the Queen. The P40 was like a sports car, fast and rugged but you felt every pot hole in the road, the P39 was like driving a Cadillac – smooth and graceful.

At the time I felt quite flashy with my mustache. The Jester picture was common amongst our crew. I never named my plane and I think the crew chief painted the Jester on this side of the plane. On the left side door we all had our fighting cocks logo which was designed by Walt Disney.

This is the logo Walt Disney designed on a napkin for the crew that stood up the 67th. It has been the official logo ever since.

67th Squadron Milne Bay June 1943

This one didn't get away. This is the landing strut and wheel from a Betty bomber over Woodlark Island that had been disturbing our sleep and making it difficult for us to take off from the bombed field. This one was actually brought down by the Cavalry unit's anti-aircraft artillery.

Collins and his second plane Merle named after his intended in Australia. I believe this to be on Munda. He flew this plane until he was killed on Bougainville.

Cockpit of my P39 with the missing compass – one of the many times the beast was under repair

I caught the baseball team flying to the Fort Knox baseball game. I am finally in a real warbird. The tragic part is shortly after this photo was taken the B-25 crashed and everyone on board was killed.

GUADALCANAL

23 July - 16 December 1943

When I got out of the Beaufighter what I had on my back and handbag was everything I owned. I tried to locate a supply but nobody knew where one was. Someone finally told me where a Marine outfit was so I grabbed a jeep and headed for that.

It was quite a ways and I was racing. The road was only a trail with the wear of heavy traffic to widen it. I came around a little curve and there was a group of people just about to cross. I couldn't stop so just whistled past them splashing mud in every direction.

In front was a short, slight man wearing three stars and smoking a big black cigar. I didn't have the slightest doubt about who that was: Lieutenant General Walter Krueger, Commander of the Sixth Army. The little German Corporal – he was born in West Prussia in 1881 and had immigrated to the US - had thousands of troops scattered around the South and South West Pacific. I figured my next stop would be the Stockade for a short stay prior to the firing squad. However I never heard anything about it.

The Marine supply man didn't have any problem with my request. I got a helmet, goggles, throat mike, flight jacket and underwear and socks with Marine field shoes. I wore the Marine jump suit the remainder of my time in theater. Those shoes were the best shoes I ever owned and I used them for 50 years. I had to get another patch from my supply when it finally got established but my big comfortable leather flight jacket went down with the ship. The Marine flight jacket was significantly lighter and actually much cooler. In some respects the Japanese had done me a favor.

The fight for New Georgia was underway in Operation Toenails and we had 3 Jap airstrips with which to contend: Segi, Munda, and Ondonga and for some reason the Japs didn't want to give up those bases.

Operation Toenails and yes that is probably the dumbest name for a combat operation ever conceived, was a joint Army Marine invasion with both services demanding close air support from any plane in the area. We were routinely diverted from our missions to handle an urgent request for air support and the same could be said for the Marine Air. One week I recall every mission was in support of only Marine ground troops.

In early 1943, Japanese defenses were prepared against Allied landings on New Georgia, Kolombangara, and Santa Isabel. There were 10,500 troops on New Georgia and 9,000 on Kolombangara well dug in and waiting for us. The strategic plan was for the Marines to take Segi Point while at the same time the US Army hit New Georgia proper and Rendova.

The Marines were surprised to find that the Japs had withdrawn from Segi and basically abandoned their airstrip. Evidently the Japanese thought it better to consolidate their assets to the north of the island and their big effort was going to be New Britain.

Once again the Japanese high command committed suicide by refusing to work together. The Japanese Army thought that it would be better to wait for an attack on Bougainville which would be easier to supply and reinforce. The Navy preferred to delay the Allies by maintaining a distant line of defense. With no coordinated command structure, the two services ran their own plans: the Navy assumed responsibility for the defense of the central Solomons and the Army for the northern Solomons.

And again I complain not. Fighting the Japanese was hard enough without them being coordinated. As disjointed as the defense for New Georgia was, the Japanese still managed to cause our guys to fight for nearly every inch of the place.

As soon as Segi was opened we flew in and started to make it ours.

The Marines fought through the jungles trying to capture the Jap life line - the harbor at Bairoko. This is where the Marines and the Army Air Forces had a falling out.

Our whiz kids sent in the 1st and the 4th Marine Raider battalions which were designed as lightly armed, high mobility, quick strike units. The Marines hit heavily armed and well entrenched Jap army units that had been waiting for them for months and they were slaughtered. The Marines withdrew and this was the first time in the Raider history they had failed to achieve their assigned objectives. The blame for the failure was placed on the lack of Army Air support which caused a sour taste in my mouth.

In mid-June when this assault was conducted we were flying 3 to 6 missions a day and we were supporting three invasions at the same time. That and the fact that our maintenance folk's equipment was sitting at the bottom of the ocean, we were trying to move into a new base with all the headaches that entails, and the wear and tear on the machines, not to mention enemy action, all put a bit of a strain on our ability to support.

New Georgia, Rendova, and Bairoko were all underway at the same time and everyone was screaming for air support. The US Army was fighting inland in central New Georgia, the Marines had taken Segi, New Georgia and were working north, Army units were fighting on the next island to the west – Rendova; and the 1st and 4th Marine Raiders were battling in Bairoko. Granted the Marines that took Segi, New Georgia had a break but they still were engaged with "pockets of resistance" as they moved north on the island.

There was no "they're just Marines we'll get to them when we can" it was this mission first that mission second and the next mission next. We didn't care who called for support we just ran support. We flew what was scheduled and we were fully booked. And the ultimate bottom line is we lost Wille McClure and Daniel Wolterding - two of our pilots - trying to support these assaults.

After staff review by the Marine Corps Brass it was determined it was foolish (not exactly the report's verbiage) to send in lightly armed Marine Raiders on a fully entrenched, heavily armed, and fully alerted enemy position where they were outnumbered 2-1 and had no artillery or tank support. It was also decided that the Army Air Forces, particularly the 67th Fighter Squadron was not to blame for the Marine failure at Bairoko.

The Japs decided to abandon New Georgia and evacuated their troops via Bairoko harbor. They left a strong rearguard and the fighting in the jungles continued until October 1943. Nothing was easy about New Georgia.

The next step was going to be the island of Kolombangara and it was scheduled to be a horror. The Japs had reinforced the 9000 man garrison and the total strength on Kolombangara was 12,600 men that had been preparing the island for over two years. The Japanese Navy and Army actually performed a joint operation and both Navy and Army aircraft flew out of the Vila airstrip and the general consensus was if New Georgia was tough, Kolombangara was going to be a downright brutal meat grinder.

The Jap Navy made an attack and was running the Tokyo Express. It was on this campaign that future president John F Kennedy's PT 109 was rammed by a destroyer and sunk. Two naval battles occurred as well: the Battle of Kula Gulf and the Battle of Kolombangara.

Kula Gulf was a strategic win for us in that the Japanese only landed 850 of 2500 reinforcements; however, we lost a cruiser for one Jap destroyer sunk and one run aground. It was a win but it was costly.

At the naval Battle of Kolombangara the US Navy had 4 light cruisers (two from the New Zeeland Navy) and 10 destroyers in an attempt to shut down the Tokyo Express running the "slot". The Japs had one light cruiser, 5 destroyers and 4 destroyer transports. The US Navy sank the Japanese light cruiser but that was the only ship lost and the Japanese landed their 1200 reinforcements on the island. Allied losses were three cruisers heavily damaged and out of action for months. For the Naval side of this battle I would give them each a win.

All of these events led the Brass to skip attacking Kolombangara. All the bombing and strafing runs, the patrolling, and reconnaissance were to no avail – we didn't go in. The island was by-passed and we attacked Munda and Vella Lavella. From Munda it would be Bougainville and that would be the light at the end of the tunnel.

Once the Japs recognized that the Allied forces had bypassed the island, they evacuated Kolombangara in late September and the first part of October. A week or two later some US engineers occupied the island and with some native help started growing vegetables and watermelons for the troops in the hospitals. The decision to bypass Kolombangara was one of the rare times the average grunt and the Brass were in complete agreement.

October came and I got promoted to First Lieutenant, which put a total of 248 dollars in my pocket every month which was a raise of 50 bucks a month. I was First Lieutenant over 2 (years of service) because of my time as a draftee and therefore was awarded an extra 12 bucks more than a First Lieutenant under 2 years of service. This was the pay that was left after the US government had withdrawn my $6.00 life insurance policy payment. I did a rough calculation one day at my old rate when I was a sheet metal worker and since there was plenty of work I had lost about 3,500 dollars a year in what I could have made and what I got paid in the service of my country. This year I'd only lose 2,900 bucks.

Collins made a big deal out of the promotion and called all the squadron together to watch me pin on my silver bars. He then assigned me as flight lead, squadron special services, squadron mail officer, squadron this and squadron that, all the jobs I already had. When I highlighted that I was already doing all those tasks he said "yea but now you're getting paid for it."

One of the missions we really didn't like was escorting transports. They were slow and vulnerable and tended to loiter over places where the Japs had lots of antiaircraft cannon. And we note that when the Japs shot anti-air stuff they didn't care if it hit the transports they were aiming at or the escorts that happened to be in the area. We always hit and ran with the fighters on heavily defended sites, the transport guys never went fast and I swear they slowed down to drop their loads.

We still did a few escorts for the bombers but most of the bombers flew faster and higher than where we could perform. As previously stated we couldn't do a whole lot above 18,000 and the bomber types routinely flew in at 20,000. Transports flew in at around 160mph and stayed pretty much between 12 and 14,000 feet. We could maintain good coverage of those birds but had to throttle down significantly to keep contact. A 2 hour mission with B25s was a 4 hour mission with C47s. I often thought those transport pilots must have very comfortable chairs to sit in the air so long, or they literally were "Iron Bottomed" or "Brass Assed" because they just kept flying.

I will make just one comment on the C47 pilots. They were without exception some of the best and bravest men I ever met. They would fly right into hot zones, drop supplies directly on our people and even though their planes were riddled with small arms and machinegun fire, would turn right around and do it again. Their cargo masters would throw food and ammo out the side door as the plane flew over beleaguered troops and in some cases were dropping from nearly ground level so the supplies didn't float 20 yards over to the enemy's side of the battle. One pilot told me the thing that made his job worthwhile was when he could hear our ground troops cheering as they were dropping supplies.

On one occasion we were escorting four C47s that were on a combat resupply of a Marine unit stuck in the middle of New Georgia under heavy attack. According to the folks in the plane they would have to go in low and there was a ton of automatic weapons covering the drop zone. I had radio contact with the C47s but nothing with the ground troops. We were assigned fighter escort for the Gooney Birds and therefore didn't bring any bombs on our center line shackles. We were expecting issues because I had a six ship element and that indicated it was expected to be a tough mission. I asked the lead C47 driver if he wanted my section to run a couple of gun runs first and see if we couldn't get the Japs to calm down a bit. He thought that was a good idea but for some reason I could not talk to the ground troops directly.

After failing to make contact with the Marines I had the transport guy call them for effect and fire control. A white smoke grenade popped near an open field with jungle on both sides. The relayed report was that the Japs were about 200 yards to the northeast of that smoke. I left two ships with the transports and ran a gun run on the wood line with the remaining four P39s. We shot up the trees and didn't seem to have any effect although the Marines were yelling good job. The

C47 driver called me to make an adjustment on our follow up run and we went 100 yards further north on our second run. We came back and strafed the reverse direction and my third ship hit something that went bang. A huge fireball erupted in the woods and whatever it was; it was no more.

The last ship finished his run and the transports leveled out right behind him throwing out supplies on short tethered static lines. I would swear they were no higher than 500ft. The supplies landed closer to the south side of that clearing than the middle or north and from what was relayed, the Marines were able to get their supplies without a lot of Japanese action. Evidently the two passes by my 4 ship element was enough for them that day.

The return flight was as dull as the flight out but we still had to keep constant diligence and we were in some respects more vulnerable on the way back than on the way out. It was often too easy on the way in and the natural reaction was if it was easy in it would be easier out, and the hard part was done – the Marines had their supplies we got a checkmark for mission accomplished. Still no one took a break on the way back. We shepherded the bus drivers into a tight formation and kept constant vigil on the skies because C47s had a hard time using the standard defensive maneuver against the Zero. Dive and pull full combat boost in a gooney bird might cause the Zero pilot to miss from laughing so hard but that was all it was good for.

I heard a story – don't know if it was true or the CO just told us to scare us but one of the fighter squadrons escorting the C47s, completed their mission, flew back to the base and at the point of departure where the C47s were going to make their own base, they got jumped by a flight of four Zeroes. The Zeroes went after the transport planes and the escort was completely out of position to help. The 39s clawed for altitude and came screaming back – a process that took all of four minutes and chased the Zeroes away, but 6 of 12 Gooney Birds were burning or going down.

If fuel allowed we circled while the transports landed – if we were too low on fuel to escort all the way back we tried to get a relief squadron over the field to escort but that was not a routine success story. I escorted transports for probably 30-35 missions escorting anywhere from two C47s / Dakotas rigged for Generals to a flight of 18 for a combat resupply. We didn't lose one to air action although several went down from enemy ground fire. They were just too vulnerable to be doing the kind of flying they did, yet those cargo boys just mounted up and went any time they were called. I think it took much more guts to get into a plane with no guns to fly over a known combat area then it did to fly fighter support. Those people were some real heroic types.

MUNDA

28 October - 16 December 1943

Munda was the main airbase on New Georgia and when it fell after 12 days of fierce fighting in August of 43, the Japanese abandoned the island. What made this base so critical was now everything was in range and we didn't need tanks to get there. New Britain's five airbases near Rabaul were within strike range as were the naval and air bases on the islands of Shortland, Choiseul, and Bougainville. I know I keep saying Bougainville was the big one for us that and Rabaul, but we knew that when Bougainville and Rabaul fell, it would be the end of the Solomon campaign and the next step would be to land troops on the Japanese home islands. Once that happened we were sure it was all over.

Munda was 200 miles northwest of Guadalcanal and when we moved up there even the short range of our birds was enough to hit everything. Munda was a big rectangular mat built by the Japanese and modified by our Seabees. It started at the ocean and ended at the foot of a slope. The hill was a gentle slope that we took off over and there was a graveyard on that slope where the Army had buried all the men that had died taking this place. Every time we took off we were reminded of the cost of this war. There were an awful lot of crosses there.

Munda had been operational under the Japs but our Seabees immediately began improving what they had started. Seabees from the 73rd and 24th CB hit the island on the 9th of August while the Army ground troops were still clearing out the Japs from the island. There was plenty of coral on the island and the crushed coral made absolutely the best landing strips in that part of the world. I read that after the war, the air strips with coral runways were turned over to the civilian administrations to use as airports and many of them are still in operation to this very day.

Munda was much the same as the work we had been doing. One thing had been added to my daily operation as I was assigned to get the mail and take ours out at the same time. The men had modified a belly tank by putting a locking door on the tank that could ride right on my centerline shackle. The mail people would put the outgoing mail in it. When I came in from my morning assignment the mechanics would hang it on the center line shackles and I would be off to wherever the post office wanted the mail delivered that day.

On this occasion the flight was to Guadalcanal about two hundred miles going down but I had an intermediate stop on the way back at our former base of Segi. The reason we didn't use Segi much was it was a short field and the field literally stopped at the edge of a cliff about 25 feet above the water. There was no abort area on the strip, you either lifted off or you were in the water. When the wind shifted you were landing in the direction of the ocean and one needed to ensure the brakes were in good repair because the strip could be short. I say could be because for the P39 there was enough room to take off and land, for the B25s, it was a bit more exciting, and the big four engine planes couldn't land at Segi.

This strip was subject to an invasion of land crabs every night, thousands if not millions of one inch little monsters migrating across that strip every single night and through the day. The heavy traffic of trucks and tractors over the strip crushed them by thousands making the surface as slick as grease. It was so slick it was common to see a soldier or Marine slip on the runway and land flat on his keister. The strip was only 2,400 feet long and was only intended for C-47 cargo planes.

Four P-38s were coming back from a mission and bad planning by someone caused them to be short of fuel. A decision was made to land at Segi. 2,400 feet is a real emergency for a 38 but it appeared there wasn't any other options. The grease on the runway made it impossible. The first guy not knowing the runway condition touched down perfectly but when he applied his brakes he slid off into the ocean. The next guy not knowing why his leader went off did the same thing.

The last two figured something was wrong with the strip and they needed to use every bit of skill to get on the very end of the strip and spend a long period rolling out so as to bleed off the speed. Both touched down on the edge of the coral and both still couldn't make it, sliding off the end of the runway onto the other wrecks piling up in the sea. No one died but it was real close and four topline fighters were lying at the bottom of the sea.

A board of inquiry ordered Courts Martial for the Flight Leader who was found guilty of not planning the mission properly and thus running out of gas. Of course changing wind speeds and directions and enemy action over the site had nothing to do with his loss of gasoline and the emergency landing situation. (I am being VERY sarcastic.)

The base commander had no reprimand as there would not have been an incident if the 38s had planned their mission properly and landed on some other strip. I always thought the base commander must have been married to at least one of the Courts Martial board member's daughter, either that or he had some very compromising photos of the board members. The flight leader was not so related nor had any photographs so he had the book thrown at him. He was reprimanded and then sent back into combat. If the board had been really vindictive they would have reprimanded him, sent him back to combat, and made him fly P-39s but there are laws against cruel and unusual punishments so he was returned to P-38s. They probably realized how ridiculous the Courts Martial was and only gave him the slap on the wrist.

My first landing there was nip and tuck. I didn't have fifty feet to spare. From then on I came in full flaps, nose high and lots of rpm. The instant I cleared the end of the strip I chopped the throttle and the ship fell down. I put it almost in the water as I dragged it in. That whole operation was a stupid affair. I yelled about it and in a couple of days they scraped off the squished crabs by using a wire roller brush. Now they didn't scrape the strip based on my yelling – but a second Courts Martial would be with the base commander and not me who had orders to land on 2400 feet. 2400 feet was too short in perfect conditions, it was drastically too short covered in crab grease.

A short time later there was another gruesome incident on Munda. There were several little Lockheed transports around, old Lockheed Lodestars. I had seen them and wondered what they were for. They could carry 16 passengers or could be configured to haul 5,000 pounds of cargo. It used the same Wright engines as the DC2 so there was some compatibility, but I couldn't understand why the duplicate mission for two distinct aircraft with the C47 being such a superior alternate. I guessed the planes were in theater therefore they needed to be used; but they were really out of date and underpowered machines as I found out the hard way.

Our parachute racks were up a little slope right at the corner of the mat close by to our latrine, which made the place a popular spot. It wasn't unusual for some of the guys to stop in the parachute shelter and watch the activity on the field and shoot the breeze when we had some down time.

This particular day there were three or four of us watching the activity on the airfield blabbing like little girls. One of the Lockheeds was coming down for takeoff and I can remember wondering why he wasn't getting off. Then I saw his left wheel smoking and I knew he was trying to abort. The left tire blew and the strut collapsed as the ship swung toward the good wheel with the brake which was holding hard. The tank must have ripped because she blew with a tremendous sheet of flame. Later I was told, that airplane's wheel struts were somehow involved with the fuel tanks.

We just stood and watched. There wasn't anything anyone could do, everyone on that plane was standing before his maker. I finally noticed the emergency units were keeping everyone a good distance back and not trying to foam the wreck. This was odd behavior for the crash crews even for total wipe outs because the field was effectively out of commission until the wreckage could be cleared. We soon found out why no one was attacking the fires. The little bird was carrying depth charges and they were just waiting for them to go off. If we had known we would have been running like madmen but we didn't.

The charges all went off together when sympathetic explosions occurred and there is no way to illustrate how violent that explosion was. The carburetor on one of those engines is approximately 16 inches square and 6 inches deep. It is bolted tight to the engine and I can't even imagine how much force is required to rip that carburetor off. We couldn't see much of the detonation because the shock wave almost eliminated us but the violence of the explosion ripped the carburetor off one of the engines and blew it up in the air so high we didn't know it was up there. It took a long time to come down and when it came down into the shelter with us it went through two racks of parachutes and on into the ground.

Those depth charges cratered the coral runway and we were shut down for a half day as the Sea Bees hauled in new coral to patch up the hole which was easily 50 feet across and 10 feet deep. There was nothing to do for the crew of course they couldn't find enough of all three to fill a match box let alone ship the remains home so we had a memorial service the following day without the remains. Turns out they were Navy folks and the Navy had purchased 100 or so of these Lockheed Lodestars. They were underpowered and the center of gravity was off so the flaps had to be set exactly right for either landing or take off and if they were reversed what happened on our strip was the normal result. There is one miracle associated with this event, other than the crew of the plane no one else was killed or injured in the crash.

On rare occasions we actually received briefings that accurately described the enemy disposition, the weather, terrain, and supporting units. Rare but occasionally we did get all the information we'd need to study and build an attack plan.

Collins had briefed an attack on a Japanese trench atop a ridge line extending east to west. Intelligence said there was anywhere between two infantry companies to a battalion on that ridge and that our ground pounders were going to take that ridge later in the day, so we needed to go in and provide support. Collins set up the attack plan and drew a picture on the ground using a stick so all could see. He had everyone refer to their maps as he pointed to various terrain features and manmade structures on his diorama as he explained the attack. He would take his element and attack the trench perpendicular to the defensive line (North to South) I would take my element and attack down the trench line East to West.

If we had practiced this attack 100 times and were given the best flying conditions and the enemy had only blanks; we could not have gotten this attack to go off half as well as it actually did. Collins had 10 birds for this run so his element made the frontal assault, my element the flanking attack and the 2 remaining birds provided top cover to ensure we didn't have any nasty surprises while we were beating up the Jap ground pounders.

Collins came in low off the beach heading for the ridge. I broke my section off and looped behind him sneaking off to the right of the defensive line. Collins' folks assumed a formation known as line abreast– each plane side by side approximately 25 – 30 yards between planes. They came roaring off the surf line 50 feet above the ground and hit the ridge square; four ships firing machineguns, cannon, and dropping bombs on the trench line. Coming off the surf the noise of the engines was masked and Collins' flight caught the Japs by surprise.

To make things worse for them – the Japs were swinging their weapons to engage Collins' flight as it flew behind them and didn't see or at least didn't react to my team's attack. Just as the last plane from Collins' flight closest to my path cleared the trench I swooped down immediately firing all my guns and cannon and dropping my bomb on anything that looked like a viable target. Before I cleared the trench my number 2 opened up and before he finished his run my number 3 commenced firing.

Again like clockwork, as soon as the last plane from my element passed the trench, Collin's reformed element now attacked from behind the Japs, coming South to North. Again the horrendous noise as sixteen 50 and 30 caliber machineguns and four 37 mm cannon ripped into the trench and anything that happened to be there.

At some point I guess you actually feel sorry for the mugs. The only hope they had of survival was to get out of the trench and make for the woods – the few that tried were chewed up and those that stayed in the trench were annihilated. Like I said, you feel sorry for them and then remember one of your buddies that burned from 17,000 feet and all the sudden you don't feel so sorry anymore.

The instant the last of Collins' team had cleared the trench I started my run back down the trench coming West to East. Again we fired our guns and cannons but there was not much moving in that trench.

Just for some overkill Collins told me to take my flight to top cover and called down the two birds that were orbiting overhead. They made a straight in run but there was absolutely nothing left to shoot at.

We caught the Japs in several mistakes - they were supposed to build a trench line in a W fashion so that the earth would prevent what my flight did to them. Straight in shots along the length of the trench were simply devastating, even misses were funneled down the trench until they hit something. Don't know how they did it but they managed to mount their heavy machineguns and anti-aircraft cannon on traverse wheels that apparently were able to bear fire either North or South but could not be brought to bear on the east to west flanks, the exact place they were most vulnerable. The last mistake they made was they hadn't built any overhead cover for their trench. Don't know if we hit them before they had a chance to build it or if they didn't know to build overhead protection. Either way as Major Hecht was fond of saying – when you catch the enemy doing something dumb, make them pay for it.

There are not many rewards for this kind of work but we did get one the following day. Seems the US ground pounders that attacked that ridge basically had a walk in the park and took no casualties. That was passed to us in the squad hut before we headed out on another mission. That meant for that one day some mother was not going to get a letter from the war department expressing their sympathies for her loss, some father might have got to go home to his wife and kid, or some sweetheart returned to the girl waiting for him. Not saying they didn't get blown away later in the war but at least for that one day; because of what we did – no condolence letters were sent home and that kind of reward we could take to the bank.

The next event of consequence happened on a day when I had the early flight. We were rousted out at 3:30 am as usual and went to breakfast and took off just before dawn. I can't recall what we did that day but we got back and found the entire squadron was down with food poisoning.

The food we ate must have been ok but I shivered when I thought what it would have been like in the cockpit if we had been poisoned. Men in great numbers were caught just as my squadron was and there was nothing to do but let the flu run its course.

Latrines were filled to capacity and men were out in the brush all around us. A few were so sick they weren't found for a day or so. People often say, "that's a mess." to describe some distasteful condition; it isn't within my ability to describe that mess. With basically the entire squadron down with the runs, I had the early flight to run the entire show. Where we would normally put up a full squadron I had two planes. Ready strip still needed to be maintained and I had to fly solo recon patrols. The few folks that were healthy on the ground had triple duty as they tried to keep the birds in the air and care for all the sick guys. It was simply overwhelming and Collins despite his best efforts was down with the rest of the squadron.

Sometime during this part of our tour in Munda I got involved in another unique experience for a fighter pilot. It was customary in the evenings for a bunch of the guys to gather at the end of the Quonset hut and play poker.

The doctor was an avid player and he had access to some kind of alcohol. The guys mixed that with grapefruit juice. Sour, sour, grapefruit juice and it was downright ugly. We'd play until lights out at ten o'clock. Ordinarily I would get my stuff laid out before getting into bed because in the morning we would have to dress in the dark – my flight having standard dawn patrol. Some of the guys wouldn't have to get up early, so, no lights in the morning to dress with.

One evening I was undressing to get in bed and had dropped my pants to slip them off. I was sitting on the side of my bed when a huge slug of a worm, dropped from the top of my mosquito bar and landed on the inside of my right thigh. It bit as it landed. It hurt like the devil was tormenting me. This worm evidently could bite and sting at the same time. I don't have a name for it.

I captured the worm and headed over to the doctor who looked at the worm and said he didn't know what it was. I was trussed up and loaded into the back of a truck and headed over to the hospital. A short time before, we had heard that a new field hospital had been set up at Rendova. This island was about straight south of Munda and about fifty miles away.

Field Hospitals are very big outfits with large staffs. They just came out from the states and seemed to know everything. Like all professional people they knew it all and most of them hadn't observed the prep required of people preparing for transfer to the tropics. They ignored the quinine requirements and hadn't taken the Attabrine as required. People didn't like it as it had some effect on skin coloring and these lovelies didn't want to destroy their sex appeal. That was how it generally went. They arrived in the Solomons and shortly a chaotic number of the staff went down with Yellow Fever.

The hospital was installed to handle the great number of wounded expected from the landings at Empress Augusta Bay. To resolve the problem while getting people to run the hospital on a temporary basis the Brass stripped all existing units of medical people. That was the situation when I arrived at the hospital that night from Munda. It was a terrible decision by the Brass.

Some kid, likely a ward boy, told me to go to a certain tent. He said 'there are some officers in there.' I did that. I walked in and I believe there were five men in there. It was a ghastly mess. Some of the men were critical. Even I could tell that at one glance. The kid had told me there wasn't anyone to look at me, so I figured I had to sweat it out.

One of the men was choking to death on his own vomit so I grabbed him and turned him over so the fluid would drain out of his mouth and throat. The other men in the tent were combat casualties. None were ambulatory.

The man with Malaria, I found out later, was in hospital for the third time with Malaria. My pain faded quickly so I was able to get the men cleaned up somewhat and got water and food to them. I found a gallon can of beans and some bacon with some bread and made coffee in a big pan. I needed that to stay awake.

The man with Malaria was the scary one. I hadn't the least idea what to do for him. He had big fever so I got some aspirin and gave him aspirin two every six hours. He upchucked again and I found one of those glass straws. I was desperate so I turned him on his stomach. I washed my mouth out and took in as much water as I could and blew water as hard as I could into his mouth through the straw. I can't believe he could have anything left in his stomach so it must have been terrible to attempt to throw up. I did that three times while I had him lying on his stomach. His mouth and throat were cleared out I believe because his breathing was improved.

The other men suffered because I had no idea what to do for any of them. Food and ordinary cleanup was all I attempted. People started to show up and two men came into the tent the second day. They said they would take over and I caught a ride back to the strip and went to bed. Collins let me sleep in the next day and the day following I was feeling good enough to fly again.

Once again as part of my daily tasks I was flying the mail back to Guadalcanal. The heat of the day would cause thunderheads to rise to great height 40,000 feet not being unusual and well above my ceiling. Heavy rain showers often occurred. Clouds would cover the sky to the extent that I would have to climb to 18/20 thousand feet to find a notch to pass through. That was a huge tasking.

One evening I didn't get away from Henderson until late. It was getting dark and was gloomy climbing out. As soon as I started to work through the thunderheads it got black, but the higher I got the lighter it would be at least for a few minutes then night would close in.

I knew there wouldn't be any lights on the ground or the water and I was beginning to think I would have to call radar for a vector. That might be the worst thing I could do because they might vector me right into a gigantic thunder head with vertical currents of 300 miles an hour. Even experienced pilots don't want to fly through thunderheads.

I was running out of time and would have to let down or over shoot my landing. When you are in a fighter and in heavy rain your vision is limited to looking out of the front quarters of the windshield. That isn't much either.

It was now black and I was convinced I had to let down regardless of the consequences. At that instant I saw a dim glow of light, which must have been a reflected light from above coming through a hole in the massed clouds. A last flash of sun light was beaming through. It was just enough for me to see a notch in the clouds and I dove for it. I leveled out at a thousand feet and I was able to see white surf on a beach. I saw the field on my first circle and put down. This event had nothing to do with luck. I know who got me back to the strip and I thanked Him for His guidance. Once again I thought about that air plane stewardess and her prayer.

There was one other event that had happened before I landed at

Henderson one evening. The spot where the mail service had me park was in a corner near an ammunitions dump. This particular day, that dump was going up (exploding) and it was everything that is frightening. There wasn't any fire at that moment just gigantic Carrumphs from the explosions. I felt the ground rumble and shake as I taxied in and after shut down the airplane almost danced it was that close. I could see great gusts of flaming debris as various parts of the base where thrown 100s of feet into the air.

It seems there isn't any way to fight a munitions dump fire. It seemed they just watched until it wore itself out, and then came in with the foam and the water. Flying the mail was a dangerous chore all by itself and I surely didn't need the added excitement of the ammo dump going off next to my revetment.

Day after day we flew up the slot. There were great numbers of SBDs and TBFs doing bombing runs and Rabaul was catching it every day. Halsey said of the Japs that 'They will never sleep again.' This was all out full blown day and night bombing and strafing involving the Marines, Navy, and the Army Air Forces. Our fighters were ground attack, the B25s were Naval and ground attack and the big boys the B-24s and B-17s just wanted to reduce the elevation of that island. We dumped everything on it.

The Japs were trying to get out of the New Georgia area and they used whatever means they could devise to do it. I think these were the remains of the rear guards on the various islands that the Japs were trying to reconsolidate. They would work as much stuff toward Rabaul as possible during the night and then go into hiding at one of the many unoccupied islands during the day, because at this time we were starting to get air superiority.

We had reports that the Japs were using any motored ship to haul barges full of men to reform at either Bougainville or Rabaul. One that apparently was getting some fame was a destroyer of a fairly new class that the Japs had installed with radar and improved the anti-aircraft weapons. Instead of the standard six 5 inch naval rifles most Jap destroyers had, this destroyer was reported to have 8 smaller guns perhaps 4 inch naval rifles and an improved antiaircraft control system as well as improved depth charge launchers, and of course it had their terrible torpedo that cause such havoc in the US Navy.

Coast watchers and recon planes had caught this ship over and over but when the strike planes showed up the destroyer was simply not there. Two Naval Venturas were reported to have found the ship with a string of tows behind it and both planes were heard going into the attack. Both planes were never heard from again and the search and rescue plane could find neither the planes nor the destroyer.

Later research indicates that this destroyer may have been of the Akizuki class and that it was loitering around the various abandoned / unoccupied islands. We thought this "phantom" would detect the planes miles out, drop her tows and race out to sea. The barges would then hide in coves and shallows and were fairly effective at moving. Of course the main movement occurred at night and we believe they hid during the day.

That we heard so much about this phantom destroyer baffled me the most. Where could he hide? Yet no naval or air search could bring this ship to bear. I settled on the idea that he would drop his tow(s) and headed straight out to sea before first light. Being very fast he didn't need much time to get over the horizon and out of sight and with radar he could "see" at night as good as any US ship. He would have used a lot of fuel but apparently that vessel had extra fuel tanks in its design.

This particular morning I was going up alone. I haven't any idea why, unless I was on a search. At the time they were building the strip at Empress Augusta and we were still working out of Munda. I was off shore several miles to the north of New Georgia when I came up on a barge. It was Jap and one of their brand new ones. It was all metal about 40 feet long and she was dead in the water.

It apparently had a mechanical breakdown and something must have happened to it so they couldn't get into hiding. There weren't many men in it and I deduced they were a working party trying to fix whatever was broke. When I went around to make a pass on it, the men jumped into the water and spread out so there wasn't any concentration of people. I concentrated on getting cannon shells down through the hatch and I am sure I put three inside the hull. The next day I made a divergence to look for it and saw it had washed up on the beach at Monatu Point and was half sunk. 30 and 50 caliber rounds and 37mm cannon make huge holes in the hulls of thin skinned ships.

I would like to pontificate for a few moments on the 37mm cannon. One of the senior pilots to arrive in Australia in the early months of 1942 outlined some awful problems with maintenance on the 39s and pilots losing formation.

Not being there, no one can criticize the Mechanics or the Supply support. They had what they had and that is that. But losing aircraft and pilots while flying cross country is not understandable. And not holding formation is not only not understandable it is unforgivable. I wish he had expanded on those two items.

His defamation of the 37mm gun is poorly based. The Russians converted to 37mms as soon as they got 39s with 20 mms guns in them. I have to believe the man just didn't take time to learn the weapon.

The 37mm cannon had a gravity cartridge discharge system. A pilot could not fire the gun while pushing the stick forward. The gun would jam because the expended shell could not clear the bolt. That rule was inflexible but the gun never failed if the pilot knew his gun. Only fire it in level flight or while pulling positive 'G's. That does not mean the gun could NOT be fired with the nose in a "declined" position, it just meant that when firing, raise the nose, stop firing, and then continue the dive. The cannon could easily be zeroed with the 30 and 50 Cal guns, at short range and in that one respect it was devastation defined. At longer ranges it would not hit where the .30 and .50s would hit. I zeroed my guns at 1500 feet – 500 yards. I fired hundreds of rounds through that gun but mostly used it alone when shooting at fixed targets and several times at barges. The attack on this barge had to be fired on with the nose of the plane pointed downward as it was impossible to get level with the barge that stood possibly 10 feet above the water, therefore as long as the plane was "mostly" level when firing the 37 mm cannon worked like a charm.

The "phantom" destroyer must have given up on the barge because with all the trouble they were having at Rabaul they knew they could never get parts for it. We ran many a search and several attacks on high confidence intelligence sightings of the Phantom but we never found it. One mission had all of our ships, most of a Marine squadron and several SBDs involved in the search for the Phantom that had been reported by the coast watchers not 4 hours old. We came screaming in at low altitude positive we had finally found the tin can but when we arrived all we found was open sea. It is one of the mysteries of the war that has always bothered me.

So it is only fair to ask why Rabaul and Bougainville were of such importance. Rabaul was the center point of the Japanese defenses, over 110,000 men were stationed on the island of New Britain and Rabaul was the main base. The Japs had taken the island away from the Aussies in early 41 and captured several thousand men. They enslaved the prisoners and made them dig tunnels and trenches in the rock and that place was basically impregnable.

The harbor had tunnels cut into the sides of the mountains so they could bring in the barges and dock them right inside the hills. They could then have their slaves unload the barges under the protection of the mountain and then distribute the supplies over the complex without ever having to go outside where we were dropping bombs. I heard there was almost 35 miles of tunnels dug into those mountains. Some were large enough that they put trucks in there and there were several elevators and stairways to move vertically up and down the mountains.

Several other things made Rabaul a formidable defensive position. The harbor was well protected by the lay of the land and the guns the Japs were able to install. They actually made gun emplacements on top of the clouds and there was a strange phenomenon when attacking the harbor, the guns mounted on the hillsides shot downward at you.

There were 5 airbases around Rabaul with another 4 on the island of New Britain itself. These planes were camouflaged and hidden in revetments and in some cases caves cut into the mountains and there was absolutely no shortage of antiaircraft weapons or ammo. Both the Navy and the Army understood the importance of the island so some of their best pilots were stationed on the island and the better equipment was stationed there as well.

Besides tunnels, there were dug out offices and squad bays and storage areas not to mention a 500 bed hospital and a 2000 woman brothel. The captured prisoners were not all men. Prisoners from the fall of Malaysia were brought in as well and some of those folk were Indian serving with the British Army. They were according to most of the readings I have made; treated the absolutely worst. Beheadings and bayonet practice was routine for prisoners that couldn't work anymore, for Indians it was not only completely random but quite frequent. The Japs treated all their prisoners horribly and were cruel and unusual in their behavior towards the Allied POWs, but for some reason had real heartburn with the Indian soldiers.

It was on a mission to Rabul that some folks in my squadron had a nasty surprise. We had heard of the Japanese plane that looked like or was a copy of the German Messerschmitt BF109 or one of the Italian jobs, perhaps a Macchi C202. It was neither but this was the first time we had seen them. The Kawasaki Ki61 Tony was just being introduced at this time and was one of the few inline engine machines the Japanese ever designed. It was as fast if not faster than us and had a service ceiling of 38,000 feet roughly 20,000 feet higher than what we could operate at, but like us it was limited performance at higher altitudes, evidently the Jap government had weenies like ours that pulled the turbos. It was heavily armed for an army plane with 2 20mm cannon and 2 .50cal machineguns. Unlike the Zero and most other Jap planes it could do two things that were unexpected, it could take a hit and not flame and it could dive with us. It had self-sealing tanks and used armor plate behind the pilot. It paid the same price for those attributes as we did in that it was a short ranged weapon; 370 miles was the max without tanks as compared to the Zero at 1900 miles. At 313 MPHs the Tony was only 17 MPH slower than our 39s.

Still it was a nasty surprise as some of our guys managed to get tangled up with a pair of Tonys. They applied our standard defensive maneuver and threw the nose down into a power dive and shoved the throttle through the firewall. There was still a moment of intense fear as the plane in this mode was exceptionally fast, but 20mm cannon shells were faster, still it was usually only for a few moments and then we pulled away from the light Japanese planes. Well the 20mm cannon and 12.7mm (.50 calibers) kept coming. One of the pilots checked his gages to ensure he was diving correctly and still couldn't figure out why he was still seeing tracers from the planes behind him.

Some of the better Japanese aces flew the Tony but the two in pursuit of our two squadron members were not one of them. The 39s dove into a cloud bank, pulled a 180 curve and swung back out of the cloud bank clawing for altitude. At altitude they were now ready for the fight but they never found the Tonys again. They rejoined the squadron on the way back to Munda and it was one of the times Collins allowed chatter on the squadron radio net.

Needless to say we had an update to our intelligence group and that blurb went out to all stations with the red border. Tony's were a real nasty surprise and unfortunately some Allied pilots were not so fortunate as our two pilots, and the Tonys got the reputation as B29 killers, but some of those kills were by ramming.

The heavy bombers worked on them at night and vast numbers of SBDs and TBFs covered Rabaul and all its airfields during the day. I can remember one time we went in to Rabaul on a daylight raid with the heavy bombers. They were B-24s and there was a bunch of them carrying a full load.

We were close cover for the dive-bombers so the heavies were much higher than we were. The high value targets - the B-24s - were being escorted by the P38s and we had the lower value targets - the SBDs which just made the Navy and Marine pilots literally leap for joy. The thought was that if we were bounced the Japs would go after the Airacobras as they were as previously noted an easy kill. On this attack the B24s attracted Zeroes and Tonys like honey attracts flies. Flight after flight of the Jap aircraft swarmed around the heavies up top and we were left pretty much to ourselves.

A Jap fighter got shot up so bad by the top flight fighters that he had to jump. He drifted down through the B-24 formation and every gunner in the squadron shot wildly at him. The crewman who described it to me said the Jap must have been a big shot because when he jumped he had a big sword or saber clutched in his arms. He was shot to ribbons when he went through the bombers. When he dropped the big knife I would think it went into the ground a hundred feet.

Sometime after that raid the commanding General, General Barnes, told Collins he wanted to take a hop in a '39. Collins told the old man it wasn't all that simple but the old pilot insisted. Collins gave him a comprehensive briefing and the General got it off. He flew around for about a half hour and decided to land. He must have got confused at that time because he could not get the gear down. Collins knew the system was ok and tried to coach the General through the simple procedure but he couldn't get the gear to move.

Collins was getting worried. He figured the old man was not using the right switch. He then tried to get the man to use the hand crank. He did manage to get the gear unlocked but the General was never strong enough to pump the gear down. In desperation Collins jumped in a ship and pulled up beside the General. That was the best move he could make. He would tell the old man what to do and flying sideway so the General could see what he was doing in his cockpit motioned to the control at the same time he was describing the procedure. The gear finally came down and locked

Collins flew down with the man and that was probably a smart move, also, because the General had never landed a plane at120 mph approach speed in his life and the gear episode had obviously rattled the old gent.

The day came when the Brass figured the Japs were softened up enough and they had the Marines go and established a beach head at Empress Augusta Bay. On our way up there that day I saw a Cruiser being towed back. She had taken some serious battle damage and was streaming oil for miles and miles.

Collins had engine trouble and couldn't go on with the mission. He told the second lead named Twitchel to take over the squadron and ordered me to stay with him. Why Collins didn't go home I don't know but he was the boss so I didn't ask. He said he was orbiting at twenty inches of mercury which was all he could get. While he was working on the problem I saw a Betty bomber go by on his way to the beach head. I had been ordered to stay with Collins so I just watched him go by. He was quite a ways out but I could have caught him.

I have been asked just how many planes I shot down and I have to honestly say I intentionally shot down no planes although I did get credit for two, both were mistakes.

My first kill was on a mission to Rabaul. We had good intelligence with high confidence that there was some shipping in the harbor. Intelligence in those days was not as clear as it is today. Intelligence simply meant someone guessed it would be a good idea if it was there.

Intelligence with Confidence means someone guessed it would be there and someone else who may have been sober but that is not a requirement might have agreed with him sometime in the last couple of weeks. Intelligence with High Confidence meant someone really thought it was a good idea, two or three guys that might be sober agreed with him AND there might be a slight possibility that a plane or ship had actually sighted something within the last couple of weeks. Nothing ever panned out the way it was briefed. Well rarely.

We were on a high confidence mission laden with bombs, full ammo trays and were hugging the island as we approached the bay. As I started to pop up to clear the saddle and dive on the bay a Japanese Nakajima B5N which was primarily a carrier bomber but was often used by the land forces as well flew literally across my windscreen. He could not have been more 200 yards away and it was clear he had not seen me any more than I had seen him. I squeezed all the triggers, machineguns and cannon and the plane disintegrated before my eyes. I never slowed or deviated from my attack run and popped over the saddle to commence my run.

My second kill was almost the exact same scenario but the other end. We again were responding to high confidence intelligence that there was a squadron of ships and supply craft in the bay offloading supplies. When we arrived we found only a couple of rafts tied to the pier and a couple of sheds where perhaps some supply may have been stored.

We bombed and strafed the harbor and then beat feet out of there. As I banked out of the harbor I thought I'd take my flight over the jungle for a few miles and then swing out to sea – hoping to throw off any Japanese pursuit that may have been alerted by our raid. I banked hard and the instant I leveled out there was a Japanese GM3 Betty – the same kind of plane Japan's war leader Yamamato was shot down in, taking off from a runway that "intelligence" knew nothing about.

Again I pulled all the triggers and blasted away at the enemy plane, I think I even hit the bomb release lever. It was so close I could see the rivets in the wings. It burst into flames and crashed in the woods. My flight and I continued our hasty retreat and later reported the general location of the airfield. It turns out that in the end the Japanese had 9 air bases on that island.

Anyway that's my huge score – it was unlucky for the Betty crew - they probably didn't make it out. The B5N guys might have landed the plane but it was pretty shot up.

My third Christmas of the war saw us on Munda preparing to move forward in January. One of the guys caught me and said there would be a mid-night Mass some place out in the jungle where they had constructed some benches and a table for an outdoor church. The "cathedral" was triple canopy with trees growing inside trees and bushes taller than a man. Vines and orchids grew randomly throughout the church and although there was no stained glass the sun showed down through the opening in the canopy with almost a spotlight effect. At midnight there would be no sun but there was a glorious three quarters moon and our gas lanterns.

My buddy said we should go and we did. Mass progressed to the Consecration and just as the Priest elevated the Host, shells started falling close to us. These were big shells and fused to go off on contact. The canopy of the tops of the trees were a hundred feet high and the Japs fused the shells to go off on contact so shrapnel and tree splinters – some 10 feet long - flew all over. The seats and kneelers were coconut tree logs probably plowed up by the Sea Bees when they built the airstrip. Men were diving down between and under the logs seeking any kind of cover.

One thing about the Catholic Church is that once the Consecration is started it will be finished. That young priest finished the Consecration without seeming to notice the shells. He had to have had nerves of steel because he never flinched while the shells were landing around us. The Japs continued to shell the area of which our little church took its share of hits. When the shelling ceased the priest continued the Mass as if nothing had happened. And that is how we celebrated the birth of the Prince of Peace in 1943.

OPERATION CHERRY BLOSSOM

1 November 1943 - 1 January 1944

Unfortunately in the fog of war, operations overlap and to the folks doing the fighting one mission in support of one operation under the command of one General and his division are interrupted by demands for support from another General and his command which are conducting another operation. None of it matters, they are all terror defined. Of course to make things worse, the enemy does not cooperate with the overall strategic plan and nearly every operation overlaps, one does not end and a second begin, rather one starts, drags out forever, and the second starts anyway which drags out and the third invasion commences while the other two are still in the works.

All this means is that support folks like our squadron were flying mission after mission with little to no relief as other than some SBDs we were the only close support in the area. Marine Corsairs were in the area but they were really needed in the fighter superiority role because as of this time in the war, we didn't have it, and the Japs still thought they were going to win.

From the end of October 1943 through the first week in January 1944 we were supporting four major operations and supporting the invasion of six islands. (That's the other part that is confusing, some operations include multiple landings and multiple attack points which for the average Joe is just simply beyond understanding.) Some invasions we knew were going to be meat grinders, but "milk run" missions got people killed just as easy as the meat grinders. You could never coast.

Operation Cherry Blossom (another strange name for an American

185

invasion) started with the US Marine's 3rd Division and the USA's 37th Division landing at Bougainville on 1 November 1943. Bougainville was going to be a meat grinder, estimates of the Japanese defense forces were between 45,000 and 60,000 Japanese army and naval personnel. The 3rd MarDiv landed and established a beach head and the US 37th Division landed shortly after on 6 November to expand the beach and develop the air fields.

The battles to expand the beachhead were extremely violent and bloody with the US Marines taking the brunt of the fighting. As brutal as the fighting was, one of the greatest casualty makers was the malaria and other tropical diseases.

We were flying out of Munda and Vella Lavella interchangeably. Pappy Boyington's Black Sheep were out of Vella Lavella and we did a few joint missions with them as well. Close air support was the call for the day and we were constantly engaged in ground support at Bougainville supporting both Army and Marine units with the priority of missions being the Marines whom the Japanese seemed to be picking on (silly Japanese).

The beachhead was expanded enough to allow for an airstrip to be built but it was mainly used by the cargo plane folks and their C47s flying in supplies and hauling out the wounded. In December 1943 the Japanese put some artillery on the high ground around the beachhead in a group of hills along the Torokina River. They shelled the beachhead targeting the airstrips and the supply dumps and were causing all kinds of havoc. The 3rd MarDiv ran a series of operations from 9–27 December to take those hills from the Japs and we flew routine support for them.

One hill named "Hellzapoppin Ridge" was a rock fortress 300 yards long, with steep slopes and a narrow crest that overlooked much of the beachhead. The Japanese built hardened positions on the reverse slopes, well camouflaged and nearly impossible to see or assault. The Marines attacked Hellzapoppin Ridge but were driven off on 12 December.

In order to minimize casualties the Marines called in several air strikes of which we were the main mission. Unfortunately our coordination was off and we missed the narrow ridge completely. Collins went crazy thinking this was yet another blame game until the second flight leader said they might in fact have missed the target.

Collins called me in and told me to load up my section and make a run on that ridge, we were to carry the 500 pound general purpose bombs and make gun runs as needed. He gave me the coordinates of the target, the Marine radio frequency and the call signs for the observer that would be controlling my flight.

We took off from Vella LaVella and pulled a tight formation and picked up an escort of four Marine F4U Corsairs, which was a real treat for us as that plane caused a lot of fear in the Japanese pilot corps, they called it the devil bird and we were just fine with the Jap air defense thinking twice before coming in to attack us. We passed over the southern part of the island and the Corsairs waved us good bye and we moved in for our attack.

I got good comm with the Marine Forward Air Controller and he gave me general directions to the ridge that was causing such grief. I evidently over flew the position so had to circle my flight around to try again. The controller said he had me in view and I was to fly north east (I have no idea and use this direction simply to describe the event). I came in low, saw nothing and unfortunately the controller was in a position where he could not see me in relation to the target.

After yet a third run I was now getting somewhat perturbed, from 500 feet I could not make out any ridge from the air, yet alone a fortified gun position which one would think would have trails and tracks to for resupply and ammo runs. From the air the area looked exactly the same as any other part of the island. I told the Forward Air Controller that I had 30 minutes of loiter time so he needed to move to a position in which he could see me and the target at the same time. He signed off and I never heard from him again. I don't know if his radio went on the fritz or he got lost moving I never did find out.

One thing I could see was the markers the Marines laid out showing where their lines were. I was running low on fuel and the loiter time was just about out when I got this idea to try and find the target by firing guns at a general area – a reconnaissance by fire if you will. Someone must have figured out what we were trying to accomplish because they threw a smoke grenade in the general direction of the ridge I assume, it all looked the same to me. My flight was as much in the dark as I was so this was a real mess.

I keyed off the smoke and fired some 30 and 50 cal at the woods. There were no secondary explosions or fires so I don't think I hit anything. I tried another pass and fired 50 yards further into the woods with the same result. I had my flight do the same taking 50 yard increments at a time but still no luck. We had no communication with the ground and we were now into our safety margin for fuel so I told my section to follow me in and drop as close to me as they could. I made a bee line directly to the place I thought I had seen the smoke and dropped, my second hit within feet of me and 3 and 4 were down right close as well.

We waggled our wings at the Marine ground pounders but by the fists in the air I make the assumption they were not too pleased with the result. I got back to Vella LaVella and reported to Collins saying I did not think we found any joy on that mission. He nodded at me and told me to get my section loaded up again we were going back because the Marines said we were nowhere close to the target.

My section loaded up and Collins had his bird and the second section loaded up as well. He was going out in a vengeance and those poor Japs on Hellzapoppin Ridge were going to pay for the insult to the 67th Squadron in particular and the US Army Air Forces in general. One would think we had never bombed a ground target before.

Before we took off he had someone on the Army side get in contact with the Marine FAC and explained to him that there would be no foul up like we just went through. The FAC was to be in a position where he could provide "positive control from approach through target acquisition" and yes we did talk like that back then.

Nine ships were in the air and we winged over to Bougainville with a real purpose. Collins called the FAC when we were in the general area and looked for a specific target. The FAC had problems identifying us at first, seems the Marines had called in Marine Air while we were refueling and they apparently missed the target as well, much to our chagrin.

Finally Collins identified the smoke the FAC party threw to orient us to the target, we got an azimuth and a distance and Collins led the way in dropping his 500 pounder on the target. He called for confirmation but his radio was out in his ship, the rest of the flight could hear the FAC calling for an adjustment but Collins had lost the ability to communicate with the controller and the squadron. I took over the bombing run and dropped my bomb off the adjustment the FAC gave me from Collins strike. I am pretty sure I followed directions but missed the target as well.

My second went in and adjusted off my hit and turns out missed by a huge distance as the FAC was adjusting off Collins strike not my strike but my number 2 thought he was adjusting off my strike. Unfortunately for me, the FAC was now getting a bit irritated that three bomb runs have yet to put any ordnance anywhere near where he wanted it. Collins of course is hovering overhead with no comm and is completely clueless as to what is going on.

My number 3 didn't wait for an adjustment, he simply put his bomb in the middle of the two strikes as he finally saw the target or so he thought, 4 followed being guided by number 3, with the FAC going crazy on the control frequency as we are not hitting anything anywhere near the target. Number 3 is ignoring the FAC saying he has a visual on the target and 4 drops on Number 3's guidance ignoring the FAC, but what 3 saw was never seen by anyone else and was not the target.

There are no hits on the fortress by the first element and I stop the second element trying to regain some calm and control. The FAC wants the second section to bomb off the original smoke but that has been obliterated by five 500 pound bombs. I tell the FAC to use one of the impacts from the 500 pounders to adjust and of course the FAC cannot tell which impact I am looking at to make his adjustment.

The second flight lead is trying to describe what he is seeing to the ground pounder from 500 – 1000 feet which of course looks nothing like what the FAC can see from ground level. The FAC attempts to get the last section to drop where he wants and for whatever reason all four bombs do no damage. It was a complete bust.

We flew back to Munda and Collins simply went over to the maintenance chief saying he needed a new radio. He went over to the comm shack in the S3's office and got the bad news from the higher ups. It was getting dark and there was no time for another mission, as hopeless as it seemed. We had a fairly depressing evening meal and no one was clowning around. For me it was especially hard as my section had missed twice.

It was decided that we would make a coordinated effort with artillery in support of the infantry attack, us providing close air support; with both the FAC and us using the same procedure to identify the target and adjust fire. When we attacked the following day, the FAC was adjusting fire from artillery shooting Willy Peter that he had the artillery Forward Observer call in. The burst of 105mm smoke round was clearly visible from 500 feet and we had positive target acquisition. We made our runs and dropped 2000 pounds of high explosive on the fortress. Finally, coordinated air, artillery, and infantry attacks resulted in the capture of that lousy hill on 18 December 1943.

My sister kept any newspaper clippings that mentioned me in the news, most of them were the same release saying I got another air medal with the dates changed, but one did have a somewhat accurate description of the schedule we were keeping. There was a delay in reporting the "fluff" news so the following article was most likely written during the January - February 1944 timeframe. I give you the Lakewood (New Jersey) Daily Times April 5th 1944 edition (from the far back page):

40-Foot Jap Barge Sunk by Aircobra (sic)
U.S. Plane Piloted by Lt Bob Case

Headquarters, 13TH AAF, South Pacific – They go right on, buzzing around like angry hornets, giving vent to their fury on anything that floats, rolls or flies. Pilots of the 13th AAF fondly call them their "peashooter," battle-tested P-39 Aircobras.

The little fighters were in the South Pacific Theatre of operations very soon after the start of the war and they're still on the job in a big way. A recent log of their activity in the air warfare of the South Pacific for one single day follows:

1. Bombed Rabaul
2. Strafed Rabaul

3. Flew barge sweeps along Bougainville and New Ireland.
4. Provided cover for C47 cargo planes all along the battle area.
5. Provided cover for Navy rescue amphibians.
6. Provided dawn and dusk patrols over Bougainville and Treasury Islands.
7. Stood by for "scramble alerts" at Bougainville.
8. Dropped bombs on various targets just for the devil of it while ferrying planes to and from bases.

Major Shelby England, 2121 Arch street, Little Rock, Arkansas, commanding office of a P-39 13 AAF fighter squadron, described the work of the Aircobras in this manner:

"We are ageing, as new type fighter aircraft takes its place in combat but war doesn't wait for the latest models. We have been doing a job."

He then thumbed through the records of the day's activities and disclosed that the Aircobras had done well.

During the day, Lieutenants Robert E. Case, Lakewood New Jersey and George T. Dubis 1100 Atlantic, Grand Rapids Michigan, had sunk a 40-foot barge north of the Tovera River on southeast Bougainville.

In a bombing and strafing sweep against Keravia Bay, in the Rabaul area, other P-39s had found a huge fuel storage area in an opening out into the side of a hill. All their bombs landed in the target area. Major O. B. Collins, 302 East Lake street, Umatilla, Florida earned credit with his flights for starting a large fire which caused a dense smoke cloud; Lieutenant Murrit

H. Davis 5601 Huberville avenue, Dayton Ohio, and his flight scored a hit that caused a terrific explosion and probably did a lot of damage.

Lieutenant Edward L. Young, Timmonsville, South Carolina, set a supply house afire at Kabagada and Lieutenant Kenneth V Uhrenholdt, 120 North Oraton Parkway, East Orange, New Jersey, blew the top off another supply house at Sperber Point. They didn't wait to see the subsequent developments.

Couple of notes here, we never called our planes "peashooters" that name was for a 1933 monoplane built by Boeing officially labeled the P26. Second admin note here is that the newspaper reporter called the Airacobra AirCobras throughout the article, the official name was Airacobra.

This article was probably written when we were at Munda and Vella LaVella as "normal" news (basically filler if you will) had to clear censors and was easily delayed by up to a couple of months. Lastly Major (later Lieutenant Colonel) England was not the CO of the 67th Pursuit at this time, later he did take over the squadron and was the one holding all the transfer papers in headquarters while trying to transition other squadrons to the P-38 Lightenings.

EMPRESS AUGUSTA BAY

23 January - April 5 - 1944

I separate this phase of the war by the naval battle that accompanied the Marine invasion at Bougainville. The Bougainville battle lasted for nearly two years with distinct phases in the battle. In the November 1943 invasion, the U.S. forces landed at Cape Torokina in Empress Augusta Bay. The bay had been chosen because it was within US fighter plane range, even our plane's range, and because the numerically superior Japanese 17th Army was concentrated at more strategic locations in the north and the south. The Marines were backed by the US Navy's Task Force 39, composed of 4 cruisers and 8 destroyers. Granted not a huge fleet but adequate for the landing on Bougainville.

When the US invaded, the Japanese made an immediate response with their Navy, 2 heavy cruisers, 2 light cruisers, and 6 destroyers which launched out of Rabaul. Japanese Navy and Army aircraft out of Rabaul and Bougainville all launched attacks on the landing force and the supporting task force as well.

The Japanese hit the morning of 2 November with their surface ships but due to significant problems in coordination, the hasty attack was a miserable failure. The destroyers launched their torpedoes at the US ships and missed and the usually highly proficient night fighting ability of the Japanese Navy was not in attendance that night. Two destroyers collided forcing both to retire from the battle and one of the heavy cruisers slammed into a destroyer causing massive damage to both ships.

Gunfire from the radar controlled US warships started to have effect and the basic result of the early morning battle was the Japanese Navy incurred more damage than they inflicted. By 5am the Japanese were retreating to Rabaul and had lost one light cruiser sunk, 1 destroyer sunk, heavy and light cruiser seriously damaged, and two destroyers seriously damaged. US casualties were 1 destroyer heavily damaged, two lightly damaged, and one cruiser lightly damaged.

This part of the battle all occurred basically at night so we did not get involved; the following morning we had everything up covering the beaches and the follow on landings as well as guarding the US shipping. The Japs may have lost the naval side of the battle but they sent over a ton of planes to interdict the invasion. I read that over the 3 days of the landings they lost 25 planes trying to hit the shipping and shooting up the beachhead. This is where we contributed; we couldn't provide top cover fighter support but we could jump any Jap plane coming down for runs on the beaches or the ships. Mostly we stood out from the ships and circled the fleet, their antiaircraft fire would cause as much damage to our planes as that of the Japanese and US Navy anti air gunners had a rep of firing first and then finding out who it was they were shooting at.

As an after note the Japanese battle fleet went back to Rabaul and was being refitted and rearmed awaiting 4 heavy cruisers and 10 destroyers from Truk to join them. The ships arrived and a detailed attack plan had been worked out (funny how when you really plan something out it works so much better). They were to launch the attack the following evening (5 November) but aircraft from 2 US Carriers - the Saratoga and the Princeton - hit the bay in the morning heavily damaging the cruisers which had to withdraw to Truk.

Every plane that could reach Rabaul both bomber and fighter hit that place around the clock as well; in the end 350 US aircraft as well as the two carriers' planes hit Rabaul over the three days from the naval battle at Empress Augustus Bay to the carrier strike on 5 November - thus ending the threat of naval intervention of the Bougainville invasion.

We were flying out of Munda on New Georgia and Renard airfields on the Russell islands. I never figured out why the shortest ranged aircraft were pulled back to the farthest away bases especially as we were carrying a 500 pound bomb on our center shackle, not a 175 gallon drop tank. When we had cargo plane escort we could mount the drop tank and get an extra 600 miles of range, but our normal load was a 500lb GP bomb.

One morning I had the early flight and it was something special because there were six of us in that flight. As usual we walked into the ops shack which was a Quonset hut. Those buildings were made of rolled galvanized steel and supported by prefabricated struts with wooden end plates having prebuilt doors and windows. I read some place a hut could be constructed from scratch by 4 men in 4 hours.

When the door was closed I flipped on the light switch so we could get settled for the dawn patrol brief. It seemed that I had switched on a barrage. I don't know where it came from – naval bombardment or one of the cannons the Japs still had in the hills, or a mortar attack which was common as well, but it was a thorough blasting. Shrapnel slammed through the building making a terrific noise and the steel used in the hut was not armor protection – chucks of shrapnel flew through it as if it were tissue paper.

I yelled for everybody to get in the ditch alongside the runway. At the same time I ran to the back of the hut where the light switch was to turn off the lights. I guess I thought the Japs were shooting at the lights.

The pilots had built a huge table out of engine crates which made it very heavy. This table was about mid-thigh high and was covered with various papers and junk that the squadron needed for operations but mainly was used as a card playing area where the entire squadron could hang out and play cards or some other game in between missions or when we were grounded by the rain. The Ops hut was a popular destination during the rainy season as it was elevated and thus dry as well as having windows cut in the sides of the metal walls so a pretty good draft of air would flow.

Just as I was turning the lights off another salvo hit and got my full attention. This time there were four shells and that is catastrophic and more shrapnel hit the shack. I was running in terror for the ditch. As I mentioned I made the varsity track team and was a sprinter by trade, doing fairly well and qualifying for the regionals. I offer no brag but when needed I could hit instant acceleration and was downright fast. I was about up to 95% of my fastest time when I hit that table with my hip and belly. I slid on my face and hands for a couple of feet picking up multiple splinters, I fully understand the damage to crews when the sailing ships of old could get a broadside into the wooden hull of another ship, the splinters are simply devastating.

I limped off the table and making the best possible speed I could I got my damaged body into the ditch alongside the runway where I joined the rest of my flight. I then thought we would be better off if we moved up the ditch to a corner where a road crossed the ditch which was away from the OPs hut. I figured the further away from the hut we were the better off we'd be. We scrambled up there and squatted as low as possible.

Soon the shelling stopped and I rose to peek over the edge of the ditch. The first thing I saw was an 11,000 gallon tanker of high octane aviation gas parked directly behind us less than 10 feet away. The driver had abandoned the vehicle as soon as the shells started to fall and if I saw it I didn't recognize what it was. I had all my men right under that potential inferno.

So far the dawn patrol was not running exactly as planned. We literally beat feet away from the tanker just to be on the safe side. The next brilliant thing I did was to pick up a large piece of shrapnel that had come to rest on the edge of the ditch. It was nearly red hot and I am sure my pathetic yelp of pain was heard in Rabaul. I wasn't feeling either smart or brave at that time. My belly hurt like sin and I didn't make the dawn patrol that day. I ended up going to sick call where the doc bandaged my arms and pulled the splinters out of my belly, thighs, and face and wrapped my hands where I had splinters and blisters from the shrapnel.

Doc said no flying that day and I headed off to my hut for some serious recoup. I got to feeling better that afternoon and made the dawn patrol the following morning. I was still sore but the pain medication – called two aspirins, which was about all we could get in the way of medical supplies, seemed to take the edge off the pain. They needed my ship in the patrols. We really didn't get much recovery time.

Collins being the good commander had a formation with his men at least once or twice a week as we were usually all over the place. Formations were used to pass on general info, red border letters, and commendations and promotions and give the commander a brief moment in time when he could check up on all his men. Collins announced he was going to put me up for an award of the Purple Heart for the wound in my belly.

Now I am generally a peaceful, gentile, type of individual. Though I've been in my fair share of fisticuffs I prefer the more sensible solution to a fracas and will only fight when pushed beyond the limits. I also attempt to think before engaging the mouth muscles. I prefer the old Abraham Lincoln wisdom of keeping my mouth shut and having people think me a fool rather than opening it and confirming their thoughts.

But as I was standing in formation in front of the entire squadron and the Captain mentioned he was going to put me in for a purple heart I blurted out that I would punch him right in the face if he did such a thing. It was a few moments later that I realized I had spoken out loud and in front of the squadron. An "ok then, moving along" was Collin's response and I was spared courts martial. I also didn't have to get that stinking Purple Heart. The Marines have a saying which I think most appropriate; the first award of a Purple Heart is the fortunes of war, second is unlucky, and third is downright stupidity. In my case the first would be ranked right up there with the third award.

I refused. What was I going to tell my grandchildren? I was running in stark terror when I incurred the wound. The Japs didn't do it. Remember old Belly Tank? He refused the medal for the same reason.

I piled up missions during that time. Commands came down that all P-39 Squadrons would transition into P-38s. All the P-39 aircraft in the command would be stored with us because until the transition was complete, we would be the only P-39 Squadron remaining active. They were all brand new planes and were P-39Ns.

So here we need another administrative note – my squadron of 27 aircraft (including spares) in the 67th Fighter Squadron was part of the 58th Fighter Group. The Group had five squadrons by this time. The 67th, 68th, and 69th fighter squadrons were all stood up by January

1941, and two additional squadrons, 311th and 314th were stood up in February 1942. All of our squadrons were equipped with P39 or P40 aircraft and were by this time being transition to the P-38 Lightenings (roughly 135 fighters plus depot spares).

Unfortunately for me – my squadron, the 67th was the last to transition to anything. But we still had to cover not only our missions but those missions of the squadron that was refitting and retraining on the P-38s. Transition took a couple of months because this was a completely different aircraft type (a multi-engine) and there was nothing compatible between the P-38 and the P-39 maintenance or supply wise.

By this time we had also learned that it was useless to send in pilots to fly ships they were unprepared to fly and it made no sense to put in aircraft into the field without the follow on support required to keep those planes in the air (note the New Guinea fiasco). So we just assumed more missions and flew more hours. The only good thing about this situation is that we had unlimited supplies of parts and maintenance equipment because we were the only squadron in theater still using the antique P-39.

One last mess was once the squadrons were transitioned to P-38s, they no longer were used as ground support. Why would the Brass spend all that money on training the old heads to fly new planes and then have the 38 used as a bomb hauler, a completely useless function for an altitude machine. Therefore, not only did we cover other squadrons' ground attack missions when they were being transitioned, when they finally came back into theater they were no longer ground support, they were fighter interceptor squadrons. I concede we wanted to do that as well but eventually the only folks providing ground support would be us and the Marines.

About this time while we still had the –D models we were called very early in the morning for a special flight to Rabaul. We were airborne in the pitch black and it was raining a deluge. The mission was a bit unusual because the whole squadron was up. That included everything that would fly and with our spare picture that was close to 24 airplanes.

There were many squadrons up at the same time, I couldn't see them but I could hear them. Some idiot cleared his guns when he couldn't see. Some guy up ahead saw the tracers going by and told the idiot exactly what he thought of that. We were all on one command frequency and would switch to our individual squadron frequency as we neared the target. Collins took us up to sixteen thousand feet and we went to oxygen (most humans need oxygen above 15,000 feet to maintain consciousness).

We were well on our way when I woke with a jerk. I had dozed off and was sliding into Collins whose screaming in my headset probably woke me up. While my adrenalin was flowing I saw I didn't have any Oxygen. I dropped down to something like ten thousand and recovered. I kept the squadron in sight and dropped my bomb with the rest of the guys. When we got back Collins had the crew chief on the carpet for not servicing the ship correctly and let him know that kind of performance would not be tolerated. The kid wasn't alone because Collins had some unkind language for me as well reminding me just whose job it was to ensure the plane I was flying was in fact serviceable and in proper order. After that pleasant little stay in his office I always had a full oxygen bottle for the rest of my missions.

Shortly after I had transitioned to the P-39N model I received some very strange orders from headquarters which involved my old P-39. I had accumulated many missions in the intervening time despite the haphazard function of my compass. Orders came down to take that beat up old antique to New Hebrides and it would be loaded on a carrier to be shipped to the States. I was amazed. What could they possibly want with that pile of junk? Out of the thousands of P-39 aircraft why select this one?

I took off and landed in New Hebrides where I found a Jeep Carrier that had been badly hurt in some recent action. She was going home to get repaired by the ship yards that built her because the facilities in the South Pacific could not handle that kind and amount of damage.

I taxied my old Number Ten up alongside the mammoth ship and shut her down for the last time. They knew I was coming and were waiting with the sling. A couple of sailors put the sling on her and they swung her through the air. I wondered if that was to be her last flight. I was left standing alone on the dock and just reflected upon the number of times that plane had seen me though the tough times. It was a lonely time for me. There can't be any way you can get sentimental about an airplane. During the several times she was wounded she always brought me home and she took care of me no matter how hard she was hit.

I was figuring I guess I should head back to the depot and catch a ride back to my base when a Lieutenant JG came out of the side of the ship and asked me to take supper with them. They were just about to eat. I stated I did not have a mess uniform and had only my flying clothes and overnight kit (a razor, soap, toothbrush and a change of socks and skivvies). The Captain of the ship was the next person to appear and he said I did not need "appropriate attire" and was welcome to join them in the mess. I happily accepted and had another big steak. That was three in a row from the Navy. I sure hit them on the right days.

I rode back to the 'canal in a B-24. This time with a regular crew and it was much more pleasant. He landed that huge monster as if he was landing on eggs and he didn't break a one.

We all had P-39-N model equipment at this time. Brand new planes. All the old -D, -K and -L models were gone. We never understood why they would give us new 39s when they were about to give us P-38s but then we grew weary trying to figure out what the heck HQ was thinking any way. We had a saying that headquarters function was to command, not to think. They probably had so many airplanes now that they didn't know what to do with them and it was more effective to have all 24 of the pilots fly the same model; supply and repair parts would be much easier on the maintenance folks. Granted the old 39s didn't have much difference between model types and the majority of the "changed attributes" were interchangeable between models but there were a few quirks and some unique parts – my super engine being one of them. I was real hesitant to give up the oversized Alison engine as I had 200 HP more than the standard D and if worse came to worse – at least 50 pounds of additional Allison armor plate behind me.

I didn't like the N model. They had taken the 30 caliber guns out of the -N model and replaced them with two fifty caliber guns in wing packs, package guns, mounted under the wings. We now had 4 .50 cal machineguns but that added additional weight that personally I never felt warranted the change. Additionally I liked the additional ammo I could carry with the two .30 cals in the wing mounts – we went from something like 1250 per gun to 875 with the .50 cal. Some pilots said the .30 was too light a weapon for an aircraft but I always figured that if you aimed at what you were shooting at you tended to hit and 30 cal was a real good anti-personnel weapon.

The most amazing thing they did with the N models was to reduce the fuel capacity in the wing tanks to provide more maneuverability. Yes I said reduce. The N's came to us with max 85 gallon internal tanks in the wings which was a reduction from our 120 gallon tanks we had in all models prior. This retarded situation was immediately resolved by a kit from the manufacturer with 4 additional fuel cells which gave us back our fuel capacity which still had the limited range.

We were only getting 650 miles on the 120 gallon tanks – the 85 gallon tanks would give us a range of 460 – 480 miles. This was absolutely the dumbest thing I ever heard. The complaint was so bad that Bell built field kits that could be installed in the wings to regain the original fuel capacity. The next dumbest thing I heard of was that the kits –at the commander's discretion, could be installed by the command's maintenance organization. This was accomplished on a Squadron level.

Once we got the additional cells mounted – which we never let any of the N's off the strip with less than the additional cells or a drop tank, we felt much better. I did mention most of our flight time was over the ocean and most wounded birds tended to have fuel issues with full capacity. Flying over 300 miles of water on reduced fuel capacity was simply suicidal.

During this period we spent some time or at least used the strip at Treasury. Each move brought us closer to Rabaul. Eleanor Roosevelt landed at Augusta Bay and toured the beach area. Of course there were a bunch of VIPs around her at all times.

All the Air Crews (all services) were quartered in one area at that time and used a consolidated mess. Eleanor was ushered in there to meet the pilots and ground crews. She asked some of the men if they had everything they needed and one man said "Ma'am. Can you get us some Bacon and Eggs?" She turned to one of the Admirals and asked "Can we do anything about that?"

I don't know how she got to the beachhead but it must have been a big ship and I would guess a carrier or battleship. It must have been over the horizon because when I landed there were no ships in sight. I had been up at Rabaul while she was visiting. How she did it I'll never know but she got the Navy to give up real eggs and real bacon. Our usual breakfast of powered eggs, spam and oatmeal was about to get replaced with the real McCoy.

Six crates of eggs and some bacon were delivered that afternoon. The crates were stacked in front of the serving counter where they were prominently displayed so the folks on the island could have sweet dreams anticipating the breakfast they were going to enjoy in the morning.

The next morning I had the early flight and we showed up at the cook's tent with a flight of Marines. We had bacon and eggs, fried potatoes, fresh baked biscuits and Jam. We left the mess tent full and fully satisfied. I think Eleanor was the only person who really knew how to fight a war.

We got back about 10 o'clock or so and there was chaos around the mess tent. The Japs had fired about a half dozen 255 mm rounds into our area and one hit square on the egg crates blowing them and the bacon to kingdom come. I understood several people were killed as well. Two flights, eight men, were all that got Bacon and Eggs from Mrs. Roosevelt

An odd event took place about this time. On this day we came in somewhere around noon. People were running around shouting 'all pilots get your flight gear and go to the landing. Double time now.' I ran out of the tent and got in a jeep jumping in next to Pappy Davis who was already seated in the back seat. We had the driver stop by the aircraft and picked up our flight gear. Whoever was driving raced down to a tiny narrow pier and dropped us off. There was a Torpedo Boat backed up to the pier and engines were racing.

Davis hit the pier ahead of me and was pulled over the transom without ceremony. I was maybe two steps behind him and the boat was thrown in gear and jumped off the pier. I threw my parachute with all my might and a sailor got that. I caught a cleat with one hand and the guys hauled me in.

The skipper of that boat would have left me if my grip slipped. I have never seen people so tense in my career. What in the devil could be going on? Why would we be leaving the planes? These questions were going through my mind because there wasn't anybody else to ask.

We hit a bow wave of a boat crossing in front of us and a titanic sheet of water rose over us and drenched everyone in the boat. I looked around and saw all guns were manned and ready. Well the current actions had me scared and as the Captain said long ago about fighting on a naval ship: There wasn't any place to hide.

This was John Kennedy's Squadron I was to learn later based in the Russell Islands which we actually had a headquarters and could have flown our birds there in an hour or so. They took us back there and let us off and we had no instruction as to where to report and what we were supposed to do. We walked from the Navy base over to the Army side and hitched a ride to the air strip where we were a complete surprise to the folks manning the strip.

I got radio message over to Collins letting him know we were on the strip at the Russell Islands. He was somewhat confused as he could look out the ops hut and see the strip and Pappy's and my airplanes were sitting on the strip on Treasury Island. I tried to explain what had happened but I could not for the life of me explain why it had happened. The next morning a cargo plane arrived and took us right back. I never saw or heard anything to explain what we had just done.

In the next two weeks we flew endless numbers of missions mostly at Bougainville but we hit Rabaul, Buka, New Britain and any place else we could find trouble. We seemed to repeat ourselves about every two days. I flew as much as eleven hours on some days. That would be three long range missions in a 39.

We had another Phantom on Bougainville that once again defies logic. This time it was not a fast destroyer or mystery plane or ghostly apparition, it was a building. And actually it was a rather large two story brick building that had been built by the friars and was large enough to house their order, the administration building and from what I recall a school and medical facility on the back end. The Japs had taken the building kicking the priests out of the place and fortified the surrounding area.

It was a fairly large compound and we wanted to bomb it several times but for some reason we could never find the thing. We thought it unfair that the Japs should have a nice brick building to live in while our guys were sleeping in the open in Monsoons. We had maps, members of the squadron had seen it on return missions and we had reconnaissance but when we loaded up to go get the place we could never find it. Collins had real heartburn with that place, why should the Japs enjoy hot running water and a roof over their head in a deluxe two story hotel when we had to sleep in tents and live like rats in the mud. Not only that but intelligence said they were using the building to spot for their big artillery cannons because at two stories it was probably one of the highest points of elevation on that island.

Someone suggested that it might be like the Flying Dutchman or one of the disappearing mines in the South Dakota Black Hills. After the war I saw a musical by Rogers and Hammerstein entitled Brigadoon about a town in Scotland that appears for one day every year from the past. They then made a movie of the musical and it was routinely played on TV. Every time I saw that movie I thought of the disappearing Mission.

It was about this time I was up alone for some reason I can't remember but the incident will only die when I do.

I was just loafing, down very low. In retrospect I'm sure I wasn't doing more than 150 mph. I was still thinking about the Mission Building and thought if I went slow and low, my vision would penetrate under the forest branches.

That was when my Post Grad Course in stupidity started.

I hadn't intended to tell this to anyone because it is embarrassing but it may have the effect of showing how we, sometimes, stumbled around and survived in spite of it.

I made several orbits around the area where I believed the building had to be but couldn't see anything. The island had triple canopy in some places and it was just impenetrable by the human eye from 500 to 700 feet.

During the several times I had been in this area I had noticed the Japs had trimmed much of the jungle down. Not cleared but thinned. I came abreast of that place and suddenly the Japs pulled the camouflage away and there were two field pieces exposed. Before I moved they went off and since I was close I could not only hear them, I could feel the vibration of the blasts. It sounded like a big steel door being slammed in an empty gymnasium and the blast rocked my plane something fearsome.

Field guns can't be elevated far but I was very low and in front so I couldn't attack the guns. I slammed everything to the firewall grabbing as much altitude as I could so I could safely drop my 500 pounder hanging on my center rail and tried to get back before they could cover the guns again. I could only have been out of sight of that target for less than 2 minutes but when I came back over the area I couldn't be sure of the exact location of those two big cannon. I dropped my bomb in an area that looked familiar and I know that was at least close.

I was pretty engrossed in the ground scene loitering over the bombed area to see if I could get any secondary explosions or see anything worthy of a gun run. Then I looked up to check my six and almost had a heart failure. The sky above me was black with smoke of what must have been dozens of anti-aircraft guns and the exploding ammunition. The Japs must have fired a million dollars of ammo at me but it was all exploding above me. It had to be that I was below the ammo's arming distance because everything went off above me. I can't estimate how much ammo they sent up but they made no hits.

I shake when I think of how many rounds of automatic weapons were fired at me. Passing close to the trees probably disturbed the Japs ability to track me. I can't think of any other possibility. I pushed over and got right on the tree tops so they wouldn't have any chance to get another gun on me. I was indicating about 350 in short order and got out over the ocean. It always seemed to me, if you got past incidences of that kind you would never do such a thing again. Getting past them is the hard part, and for some reason I kept getting into those situations.

I never saw a P-38 in all the time we were flying over Bougainville. They must have brought all those planes into Espiritu Santo on a ship and were checking out down there and must have had some issue with getting back into the fight. Our high cover was Marine air and we continued our ground support roles. When we couldn't get any high cover Collins simply brought another two Airacobras with the attack section and let them fly high cover.

A raid warning sounded and everybody ran for shelter. The pilots always built the shelter for the Squadron commander, where ever we went. It was always big, deluxe and strong. Some of us would always get in there with him, during raids, in case he wanted something done outside the shelter.

I was just getting ready for bed when the alarm sounded. I said; "I don't care. I'm going to sleep in this bed tonight. I've had my fill of false alarms anyway." I was stripped to the skin and a couple of the guys grabbed me and dragged me out. Apparently there was not going to be a repeat of the Hecht incident.

We got to the shelter and a couple more guys gave me a very hard shove down the entry way. Now all the soil around there was volcanic ash and if you've never experienced it, the ash cuts like a million sharp pieces of sand paper. I went sliding down on my belly and ripped it up yet again. It seems Collins was determined to pin that horrible Purple Heart on me. The Japs never did as much damage to me as my friends did; they just scared me more.

When we got the all clear I went to sickbay and had the doc bandage me up. I got the standard medicine for pain and washed the two aspirins down with some stale water. As I was not the only causality from that little raid but was not the most seriously injured I got to wait while the real WIAs got treated. By the time the docs got to me I had missed most of the night's sleeping time and naturally had the dawn patrol in a few hours. I finally got back to my bed and settled in just as the duty NCO came by to wake up the early flight.

They worked us to the limit during that period and the Japanese had some things to say about our flights as well. Every once and a while the Japs would shoot at our ships taking off. Mother Baily caught one on the actuating linkage of his right aileron and that was the only hit I heard of; however others swore they could hear rounds passing over or under their planes. The Brass ignored the gun but of course they were in an office somewhere.

There was a man, a Major, coming toward us and we discovered he was newly assigned to the Squadron. He was the new intelligence officer - we never had one of those before and I already have expressed my thoughts on the "intelligence" we used to get. With the new aircraft coming in I guess the 13th AF was upgrading everything. The Major was a good man and tried to do the best he could with the limited assets he had and the first brief he gave us was a real professional deal complete with overhead projector and large scale maps. We never knew just how much we had missed not having a real intelligence officer. He still never gave us anything useful but he did it so professionally.

Dumas and I were on a patrol somewhere off the Shortland islands simply tooling around looking for something to shoot up and or bomb when we got bounced. We were in a two plane element when a Japanese float plane bounced us firing its rear machinegun at us. This appeared to be what was code named a Pete. It was a biplane with a speed of about 230 MPHs and three 7.7 mm machine guns. Two fixed forward and one for the rear observer.

Normally a single float plane would not be bouncing two P39s, and it if did it would use the forward fixed guns which are more stable and twice as many as the rear observer had. We figured the Jap pilot was blind and simply ran into us. Of course what is left unsaid is how did a Jap float plane get into the bounce position without us seeing it in the first place? That part cannot be explained as both George and I were running our visual sweeps, and of course we were on assignment to actually find something to shoot up. The only excuse I give is that we were not in the expected contact area, and the two of us running into the float plane with all three parties being surprised is simply due to the fog of war.

I told George to stay on my wing and I was going to curve around to engage this guy's flank, because even though the chance of a hit by a 7.7 machinegun from the observer was slight, it only took one hit in the right spot to cause all kinds of problems. We both banked and started our swing when I noticed we were not the only planes in the area and three Zeros were coming down to pay us a visit.

George picked up the enemy top cover coming down at about the same time and started screaming break break into the radio, I called back that I had seen them and we flattened out and pushed the throttle through the firewall. At this point we had two options, we could bank into a dive and apply combat boost, or we could flatten out the turn, apply combat boost and dive. The common element in both scenarios was dive.

We both pulled combat boost and George and I cranked in a 40 percent dive on top of the combat boost and throttles to the wall. With all of that we moved out of the area in a very quick manner, and because the Zero was so light, even in a dive they could not keep up with us.

Three Zeros and a float plane against two P39s was not an even fight, and was not even a fight with the Zeros at altitude, they would slaughter us; however, we did have the advantage of choosing when to fight, so we chose not to fight at that exact moment and headed out over the sea. We continued our dive from about 14,000 feet and high speed exit until we were somewhere between 300 to 500 feet above the ocean where we leveled out and pulled back the combat boost. Once clear, we climbed for altitude and headed back to the scene where we had been bounced because we didn't like getting bounced by a float plane and if we had the altitude we could make a jump on the four Jap planes hopefully before they could see us. The plan would be to drop the 500 pound bombs into the sea and then throwing in combat boost again make yet another diving pass on the planes firing everything we had. George would take the tail Zero and I'd pick up one on the flank, the float plane was our last priority.

Sometimes we don't really think all that clear and definitely don't think with the rational part of the brain. We had been forced off the playing field and now our blood pressure was up and we wanted some payback, so we roared back at about 17000 feet looking for a fight and couldn't find the planes. We made a sweep of the area looking for anything now because it didn't matter who we fought, just so long as we could revenge our hasty departure. Still nothing. Where ever those planes went we could not find them.

George highlighted that the fuel was in the "turn back and go home range" so I led us over known Japanese occupied territory, dropped our bombs and headed back to the barn. It was a long drawn out flight that resulted in a complete waste of everyone, including the Japanese's, time.

It is also one of those missions that could have gone drastically wrong and George and I pontificated upon our good fortune that it was the float plane that bounced us rather than the float plane and the three Zeros. How all of us missed each other is one for the mystery books but there was no rationale for it. We got back to the base, made perfect three points on a clear and sunny day that had yet to become unbearably hot and pulled off into the bunker stands. We had no other run scheduled and two others had the flight readiness detail so we headed into the ops shack, made our reports and headed off to the hooch for a rare midday nap.

George and I were walking from the Ops shack when we noticed Ed Young was coming toward us. He stopped in front of us and the tone and pitch of his voice was odd when he asked 'have you heard about Collins?'

I was suddenly speechless. Ed said: "He augured in at Vunepope. The guy that was flying wing said he dropped his bomb and the wings folded, his bomb exploded and the plane hit in the same spot."

I can't remember anyone saying anything else.

A few days, before, a new major had come in to relieve Collins. Collins had worked out a deal with the General for the General to cut orders sending he and I to the CBI (China, Burma, India) theater at our release here where we would get P-51s and Collins figured we deserved that after our trials in 39s.

The new Major was polling all the men who were up for rotation to get them to stay another tour, despite the fact that we had already had two extensions because of the other squadrons transitioning to Lightenings. Only one man agreed to do it, so the new Squadron Commander was "slow" on notifying us that we had transfer orders. Still we didn't know any better so we just mounted up and flew our missions until our reliefs came, which never happened as they were pulled off to transition units.

One of the clerks came up to me and told me my orders were up at Headquarters. The new Major was holding them back to get time to work on the men who were going out. I was still sick with shock of the news about Collins. I picked up my orders at the HQ and the man passing them to me had to shuffle through a stack of them, my orders were right below Collins orders, we had been released from combat and order back to the States nearly ten days before I picked up my orders. I got a ride up to my tent and stood there trying to think what to do.

Finally I got my B-4 bag and threw everything I wanted to keep in there. The rest I left in a little heap on the floor for those not yet leaving to use as they saw fit. I got back to the Flight Line and looked around. There was a Med Evac sitting there so I walked over and asked a nurse if she had room for me. I was so mixed up at that time I never even said goodbye to anyone. I wrote letters later explaining why I forgot the rest of the men.

She said "plenty of room and you can use a bunk if you like." At Guadalcanal they put me on a C-54 where I stayed to Hickam Field, Hawaiian Islands. Toward the middle of the long over water flight we had to make a refueling stop. While it was Christmas Island on the way down it was Canton Island on the way back. That might have been just the opposite. The crew made a horrible landing there and we thought the plane was going to go up in a fireball. Needless to say, men that had survived a full tour (or tours) fighting the Japs did not want to get killed on the way back to civilization. The crew locked the cockpit door and wisely stayed inside until we had deplaned for refueling.

My Brother Dave was on Canton sometime before my arrival there when a submarine fired some shells at the oil storage facility there. Dave was hit in the back by a piece of shrapnel when one of the oil tanks blew up. There was a mix up of dog tags and my family was told Dave was dead. His wound was bad and he spent a long time in various hospitals before being shipped home, but I was able to check on him before I left.

My eldest sister who acting as the next of kin for her three bachelor brothers got two telegrams in one week saying my two elder brothers had been killed in separate actions. I found Dave in the hospital and Henry back at Pearl Harbor working as a mechanic on the big boats, his destroyer having been hit by Japanese air attack and was severely damaged beyond repair. He was evacuated to a rescue ship and the destroyer was "put down" by our own forces. I remember him saying most of the crew could not watch their ship being sunk and the gun crews on the destroyers doing the firing had zero enthusiasm for the sinking. Not once did any of the gun crews cheer when a hit was made.

Back on Canton there was a crew change for the transport which made some people feel better. The takeoff and follow on flight was a dream, the plane was expertly handled and the pretty stewardess was handing out cokes and sandwiches as fast as we could down them.

The C54 Skymaster was spacious and had deluxe seating and foot room and was as comfortable as the civilian passenger lines. The version I was flying in had a capacity for 26 passengers which was later converted to haul 50 folks, not quite as comfortably as our 26 passenger version. The ship had a range of 4000 miles which meant we could make one transit where in a smaller plane (DC2 as an example) we would have to make numerous stops. With a speed of 275 MPH it was almost as fast as some of our big bombers. Although used from 1942 through the end of the war by both the Army Air Forces and the Navy, it never came to fame until the Berlin Airlift in 1948 where it did exceptional service.

The landing at Hickam Field was a horror. The guy brought it in at too steep an angle and he drove it right into the ground. The four engine C54 bounced so high that I could read the number on top of a great hanger off the side of the runway. Rookie pilots in Ryan Recruits landed better than that and this was supposed to be an experienced crew. The plane was not designed to be bashed up as much as a primary trainer and supposedly this experienced crew was well beyond the Ryan phase.

The only thing the pilot did right was go to full throttle to gain more speed and enough lift that the aircraft wasn't smashed. He pulled up and circled the strip and set the plane down in a much more orderly fashion. Finally he got it stopped and the crew again locked the door to the flight deck. I imagine they had heard the remarks about the landing at Canton. The door was solid so the crashing fists and strong language didn't quite penetrate the cockpit but I imagine they were shaking in their boots. As a courtesy before the cockpit bashings started some of the passengers escorted the young stewardess off the plane. Then we threaten to mutilate the flight crew. I never did see them after that.

I have wondered many times why I always had trouble when riding on transport planes. I have been bombed, shelled, mortared, machine gunned, hit with cannon and shell and the scariest part of the war always revolved around a transport plane. I have flown planes with wings coming off, no oxygen, blown tires, damaged struts, blown cover hatches and never landed as rough as these fully operational perfectly maintained transports. I note those folks that flew the C47s over the troops to resupply were exceptions to our wrath.

THE U.S.

My plane was landed at Hamilton Field, San Francisco. This time it was crewed by Army pilots and that fellow greased it in so it wouldn't have awakened his passengers if they were asleep. In fairness to the civilians: many were pressed into service with little to no training on the big aircraft that had to be flown, almost on an emergency basis, at the start of the war.

At Hamilton I met with another depressing sight. There were P-63s lined up by the hundreds with Russian Red Stars on them. Our guys were flying aircraft that were old when the war started. I will always attribute the death of Orville Collins to that fact. He was the best and should have had a P-63 before any Russian.

I flew 167 missions on that tour which was the most in our squadron. I don't know why that happened. I do put in reference that the US pilots in Europe were rotating back to the States after 50 missions and they were automatically promoted to the next rank.

If Major Collins had returned from that mission and he would have gone home. What a blessing it would have been if he had brought, beautiful, little Merele home to his mother, but it never happened. The fact that we should have been rotated out of there 10 days prior to Collins going in is something I had a very hard time getting over.

I went home for thirty days and had a huge reception. My elder sister had saved up all her ration coupons and planned a huge feed with all the neighbors and as many of my high school friends in attendance as she could find. She saved those coupons for months and had purchased some from her friend and went to the store and bought a special treat

- several tins of Spam. I just didn't have the heart to tell her I had Spam every day sometimes three times a day and was quite sick of Spam. Still it was a great success and it dawned on me just how 'global' that war was, everyone – in the battle lines and on the home front - was doing what they could to win.

I didn't know any girls so I just wandered around by myself in the beginning. It was a nice evening and I decided to go to the movie. A couple walked past me with a boy perhaps nine or ten years old. I saw him looking at me and when they got a few yards ahead of me I heard the boy excitedly say, in his best stage whisper, " Mama I know who that is, He was in the News Paper. He's the aviator who sunk the ship."

He wasn't quite right my bomb damaged the thing but George's broke its back, but I decided to let the misinformation pass.

I spent a happy thirty days with my sister and her family. Then I went to Atlantic City to the Replacement Depot. Next was Alexandria Louisiana and Pinellas Air Field where we had P-39s, but were transitioning to P-40-Rs within weeks.

That was a humble excuse for an airplane because it was put together, we were told, with the left over parts the factories had accumulated when production was stopped. The brakes were no good and could never be relied on. Among all the things I never understood this was the most confusing. Why couldn't they make reliable brakes? Other P-40s had them.

Then we got P-40Ms, the Cadillac of P-40s. We got the last P-40s to be built and they were a dream to fly. That was a beautiful ship but never went any place but the junk yard. All this occurred within two months, it seemed we were transitioning to a new plane every other week. Finally we got P-51D-35s the most beautiful airplane ever built. It could and would do anything that war required.

One thing about Pinellas, Army Air Field was that all the pilots in the group were returnees from combat tours. Most were from the European theaters. Several were Aces which led to an embarrassing situation for me. Most of them didn't have 500 hours flying time so were listed as 'Junior Birdmen.' Junior Birdmen were restricted from making cross-country flights unless accompanied by a pilot – a senior - who was ruled to be qualified. In Europe they rotated when they had fifty missions and routinely did not have more than 150 hours of flight time. And as stated, the air commands over there made their rotating men Captains when sending them home. Beside the problem it caused it was totally unfair but the Brass never corrected it.

My Ops Officer was confronted with the problem. He solved the problem by assigning all the Junior Airmen to one flight which was assigned to me as the Senior and the other Senior Lieutenants to the other three flights.

Over and over I was assigned to lead cross country flights composed entirely of Captains who did not have enough hours to qualify as Senior pilots. I was a First Lieutenant and as senior pilot had command of the flights even though I was the junior man in rank. I once had to fly a cross country flight with a Major who had one third of my flight time. It was a very uncomfortable arrangement that resulted in the Inspector General from the Third Fighter Command coming down to investigate.

When I joined the 409th Fighter Squadron I was briefed that this squadron always flew with a full load of ammunition. The squadron had a mission to respond instantly if there was danger to the Panama Canal. It made no difference where we were at such a time. The strange part was with drop tanks we could possibly get to the Panama Canal but would be out of gas when we arrived. Arrangements had been made with the Mexican Government to service our aircraft while we were enroute to Panama. This standard operating procedure led to an almost tragic incident.

I was assigned to lead a flight of sixteen planes to Fort Brag. We were to perform some sort of exercise with the soldiers. When we got close to the field I suddenly saw a large formation of fighters. I could see their markings as they banked into a turn and was stunned to see they were Nazi fighters. How they got here I haven't a clue but I heard the Germans might have an aircraft carrier and Fort Bragg – though inland was within range of a strike from the sea. How they got here was really not a concern for me – they were here and other pilots were confirming them as aircraft belonging to a hostile nation. There were explosions and smoke on the ground so Bragg must have been taken by surprise.

I responded instantly, as I would have done in a combat zone. "Ready Gun Sights and Guns. Go to a full tank. Drop tanks prepare to engage!" I commanded on the radio. Even though I had senior officers in my flight I was flight lead and we were going to get some Nazis. I switched freques and called the tower saying "We have German fighters in sight do you have anything for us? We are starting our attack."

They came back with "no." and I cleared the flight hot. Just as we started to go in a voice came on the net screaming "Abort! Abort! They are friendlies." Now I know Germans that speak better English than me and that could have been a dupe but those fighters were not reacting to our attack. We safed our guns and orbited until the tower called us with authenticated instructions to land.

We secured and landed. I was met by some hostile people. It turned out the German fighters were our old A-36s dressed up to resemble German-109s. I'll give them credit for a good job. They were making a movie with Wallace Barry as the main star, and they nearly got some real authentic combat scenes.

At that time there was a procedure in being directing all pilots to check a document called Notems for Airmen. Pilots were ordered to read and initial before a flight indicating that the pilot had read the instruction and that he had complied or would comply with the instruction. It was intended to alert pilots that some unusual condition could be expected or that some nonstandard procedure was required prior to or during a flight.

A Hollywood production over our intended flight path would make front page Notems. Someone called our operations and confirmed my statement that I had complied with all posted Notems and there was no posting of a simulated German air force along our flight path. The current directive hadn't been posted by the time we had launched and that saved me from a serious Courts Martial.

My Ops officer was a Major who did his combat tour in Italy. He had played on the football team at the University of Tennessee and was a rough and tough individual not the least intimidated by the Inspectors. He told the Inspectors exactly what he thought of a system that could initiate such a situation as me and my current flight duties.

He told them he had assigned me to a position where it required me to be promoted. He went further and said I would remain there until they relieved him of his position. Nothing happened so we stayed like we were.

Another unpleasantness grew out of that situation. The next two Squadrons got all the men who were in my situation promoted and that helped in the date of rank situation somewhat however I wasn't promoted.

I didn't know it but my group commander was furious. One afternoon all work was stopped and orders were issued for every officer in the group to report to a warehouse. That was a mighty big gathering and I reacquainted myself with Captain Bill Harris, the pilot who had the snake in the cockpit in New Guinea who was the Commander of the Squadron next to us.

The group Commander was Lieutenant Colonel Westbrook who led the P-40 squadron in the strike at Recada Bay. There is a poem called 'The Rape of Recada Bay' written by one of the pilots that was somewhat famous in the States in 42. We had heard much about that strike when we arrived at the 'Canal and I got to meet him as well.

There were two enlisted men remaining in the warehouse and the Colonel ordered them out and used rotten language in doing it. We now knew this was going to be grim. We all tightened up at that. Absolute silence prevailed. (I will not use names now).

The Colonel called my Squadron Commander to the floor. He was a Lieutenant Colonel

The Colonel was abrupt. "Why wasn't Case on the promotion list?"

My CO said "Sir I didn't think he was ready."

The Colonel raged. "My Deputy and I went over his record." Do you know what we found? He has never had less than Outstanding from any of his commanders until he had the misfortune to meet you. He has more combat flight time than any other three officers and he's not ready??!!! Colonel when you leave here you will go back to your office and you will not leave that office until you write a letter to the General Commanding Third AF saying you made a grievous error in the recommendation and then you will request authority to resubmit."

Needless to say I was red faced. I had no idea the CO was going to do this and I tried to become very small. My CO was as red faced as me and left the building in a rapid pace. He resubmitted my name for the promotion and apparently as soon as he did that he was relieved and shipped off someplace, I know not where.

The air force had initiated a policy that anyone who had less than two years retainability could not be promoted, so before I could be promoted I had to reenlist in the active Reserve. I stayed in the Reserve and was immediately promoted to my correct rank.

My wartime experiences ended a year and a half later with no events worthy of mentioning. We did air shows with Hollywood Starlets –some who later became big names on the silver screen most who did not, did war bond drives although everyone was more interested in the aircraft (and I can't blame them) and stood on the stage with various movie stars and singing groups. One show very interesting to me was the show where the survivors of the men who put the flag up on Mt. Surabachi were presented. I had seen the famous flag raising photo by Joe Rosenthal just as almost the entire nation so meeting those folks was quite the treat.

We had one last tragedy which should have been a good time but was ruined by events. In my spare time I finally joined the command baseball team and ending up pitching for the area championship team. I could hit pretty well so I was Babe Ruth junior – they moved me to right field so I could bat more but I still pitched some of the games.

We had beaten the locals and any nearby teams so the captain of the team asked the base commander if the baseball team could fly to Fort Knox to play a couple of games against the Army Tankers. All was arranged and the team loaded up in a brand new B-25 configured to haul passengers. I had a mission to run and would catch up with the team upon completion of the training flight. I caught the team and did a roll over the bomber and the copilot took my picture out the window.

We landed and played a pretty tough series against a couple of tanker baseball teams- I think we split the wins. It was a lot of fun and we were the big event on the base, all the student tankers and the commands stationed at Fort Knox were represented at the games.

After the games we headed back to the field and I took off, the B25 took off an hour or so later and crashed into the trees killing everyone. Someone found the copilot's camera and sent it back to the squadron for processing. Generally when something like that happened we developed the film before sending the personal items home to ensure there was no classified or embarrassing items on the film. The clerk who developed the film knew who was flying the P51 and gave me the photos of my plane. It was a sad event.

I have tried to estimate how many active missions I flew out of my 167 missions. I had about 500 hours of flight time and I had about 120 missions when I had to fire my guns. I fired thousands of rounds of ammunition, dropped about 45 bombs, and fired several hundred cannon shells. I participated in sinking one Jap destroyer, two large self-propelled barges, dozens of towed barges, and uncounted gun emplacements. I shot up two enemy planes in the air and several on the ground. I had two missions where I incurred serious combat battle damaged and I came back several times only because of Divine Intervention.

I thank God for letting me come home.

END

ABOUT THE AUTHOR

TV journalist Tom Brokaw's book "The Greatest Generation" is the story of a generation born during the "Great War" who survived the Spanish Influenza, the Great Depression, and fought for freedom in a global war. To quote the author – "these men and women fought not for fame and recognition, but because it was the right thing to do. When they came back they rebuilt America into a superpower. No other society in history ever produced such a generation."

Robert E Case was of this generation. He never thought he was anything special. He flew 167 combat missions against the empire of Japan in an antiquated underpowered aircraft against a numerically superior, better trained, and better equipped enemy and never once thought that what he did was anything special. He flew and fought when the United States was not winning, the enemy was not defeated or strangled by lack of supply, and the outcome of the war was unknown – yet each morning he climbed aboard his P39 Airacobra and took to the skies – and there was (according to him) nothing special in that.

Robert was awarded 13 Combat Air Medals and the Distinguished Flying Cross – if you asked him why he was awarded the Air Medals - his response was that he ate his oatmeal; if you asked him why he was awarded the DFC – he would say it was because he didn't complain about eating his oatmeal.

Made in the USA
Lexington, KY
30 October 2017